# ECO-sex

# ECO-sex

## Go GREEN Between the Sheets and Make Your Love Life SUSTAINABLE

STEFANIE IRIS WEISS

TEN SPEED PRESS
Berkeley

# FOR MY LOVE.

Published in the United States by Ten Speed Press, an imprint of the
Crown Publishing Group, a division of Random House, Inc., New York.
www.crownpublishing.com
www.tenspeed.com

Ten Speed Press and the Ten Speed Press colophon are registered trademarks
of Random House, Inc.

Library of Congress Cataloging-in-Publication Data
Weiss, Stefanie Iris.
Eco-sex : go green between the sheets and make your love life sustainable /
by Stefanie Iris Weiss. — 1st ed.
  p. cm.
Includes bibliographical references and index.
Summary:"By renewing their passion for the environment and sustainability, readers
can renew their sex lives and relationships, by rethinking lingerie, birth control,
bedsheets, roses, sex toys, green dating sites, and more"—Provided by publisher.
1. Sex—Environmental aspects. 2. Sex toys—Environmental aspects. 3. Green movement.
I. Title.
  HQ23.W455 2010
  613.9028'6—dc22
  2009040409

ISBN 978-1-58008-118-4

Printed in the United States of America on recycled paper (100% PCW)

Front cover photograph copyright © Solovieva Ekaterina/iStockPhoto
Author photograph copyright © Josh Orter
Design by Chloe Rawlins

10 9 8 7 6 5 4 3 2 1

First Edition

# contents

ACKNOWLEDGMENTS . . . . . . . . . . . . . . . . . . . . . . . . . . . . vii

INTRODUCTION Feel Like Makin' Love (on a Small Planet):
An Eco-Sexual Manifesto . . . . . . . . . . . . . . . . . . . . . . . . . 1

## PART 1 🌏 Eco-Courtship: How to Green the Dating Game

CHAPTER ONE Everything You Always Wanted to
Know About Eco-Regulation but Were Afraid to Ask . . . . . . . 16

CHAPTER TWO Eco-Gorgeousness: Much More
than Skin Deep . . . . . . . . . . . . . . . . . . . . . . . . . . . . . . . 27

CHAPTER THREE Eco-Fashion: What to Wear
Until Your Clothes Come Off. . . . . . . . . . . . . . . . . . . . . . . 54

CHAPTER FOUR Eco-licious Aphrodisiac Foods:
The Cream of the Crop. . . . . . . . . . . . . . . . . . . . . . . . . . . 67

CHAPTER FIVE Are Diamonds (and Chocolate
and Roses) Really a Girl's Best Friend?
Giving the Gift of Love Responsibly . . . . . . . . . . . . . . . . . . 96

## PART II 🐦 The Nuts and the Bolts of the Birds and the Bees: Eco-Sex Is Healthy Sex

CHAPTER SIX Sexual Healing, or Big Pharma vs. Your Big O: How Naturally Healthy Lovers Ditch the Little Blue Pill in Favor of Green . . . . . . . . . . 108

CHAPTER SEVEN Make Eco-Sex Safe Sex: Birth Control and STDs. . . . . . . . . . . . . . . . . 128


## PART III 🌍 More Eco-Sexy Options for the Ecological Adventurer

CHAPTER EIGHT Looking for Mr. (or Ms.) Goodplanet: How to Find and Keep Carbon-Neutral Love. . . . . . . . . . 148

CHAPTER NINE Eco-Babes in Toyland: Green Playthings for the Bedroom . . . . . . . . . . . . . . 160

CHAPTER TEN Bed, Bath, and Way Beyond: Eco-Sexing Your Boudoir . . . . . . . . . . . . . . . . . 171

CHAPTER ELEVEN The Eco-Parenting Movement: Now That You're Plus One, You'd Better Make Green Your Mantra . . . . . . . . . . . . . . . . . . 187

CONCLUSION Burning Up for Your Love . . . . . . . . . . . . . 197

APPENDIX Your Eco-Sex Toolbox: Resources for Greening Your Love Life. . . . . . . . . . . . . . . . . 204

ENDNOTES . . . . . . . . . . . . . . . . . . . . . . . . . . 208

INDEX . . . . . . . . . . . . . . . . . . . . . . . . . . . . 211

# ACKNOWLEDGMENTS

I am deeply indebted to a small army of enormously supportive associates, without whom this book would have been impossible. My great thanks to Cheryl McNeil, whose research skills are the best, bar none. To my East Coast–West Coast team of assistants, Angela Elia and Liz Barlow, you totally rock! To Patrick Duffy for his terrific analysis and for giving the book his expert environmental imprimatur—thank you so much. Enormous thanks to Bill Katovsky for his expert brainstorming and initial feedback on this project. And tremendous thanks to my wonderful editor, Lisa Westmoreland, for making the process so much fun. Much love to my darling friend, the übertalented Peter Elofsson, for his brilliant hair and makeup work on my back-cover photo. Finally, love and endless gratitude to my friends and family for putting up with my incessant talk about keeping it green.

*I can remember when the air was clean and sex was dirty.*

—George Burns

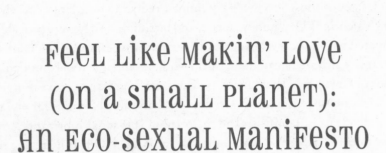

# Feel Like Makin' Love
# (on a Small Planet):
# An Eco-Sexual Manifesto

You drive a hybrid. Your home recycling system is state of the art. You buy nothing but organic produce. You're oh-so-good at being green—at least that's what you tell yourself as you carry home your "I Am Not a Plastic Bag" tote filled with nontoxic goodies. But here's the dirty truth: If you haven't thought about greening your sex life, you're still a total environmental disaster. Your compost heap isn't worth dirt if your bedroom is a toxic waste dump. Sex can be one of the lowest-impact forms of entertainment (and exercise) on the planet, but only if you do it right. Green sex doesn't have to be clean, vanilla sex; it can be as kinky as you please. But if you want it to be *good* sex (in all senses of the word), then it's time to make your love life truly sustainable.

What's wrong our sex lives? Let's start with condoms. Prophylactics often get tossed in the toilet after use, where they soon make their way into the sewers and then the water system or ocean. The same goes for excreted birth control pills, which affect marine life (not to mention wreaking havoc on your body's own ecosystem). And what about those lovely long-stemmed red roses you give or receive on Valentine's Day, anniversaries, and birthdays? They were probably treated with cancer-causing pesticides that are banned in the United States, cultivated by underage field workers, and flown in from Ecuador or Colombia. That's not very sexy, is it? Standard sex toys contain toxic, carcinogenic plastic. Used nonrechargeable batteries for vibrators end up in landfills. The majority of "personal lubricants" are petroleum based, and who wants to support Big Oil while trying to reach her own Big O?

## One Hot Mess

One of the best reasons to become an eco-sexual is that, if you don't, in a few decades you might not have time for sex—you'll be too busy searching for food or escaping from coastal flooding, hurricanes, drought, and general blight. Yes, it is that dire. Global warming (increasingly referred to as climate change) is no joke, and *peak oil* paints a *Mad Max*–like scenario that would instantly kill anyone's libido. Wanna stick around long enough to find new paths to pleasure? Then consider this: Climate change is now a certifiable threat to the national security of the United States. According to a

PEAK OIL: The point in time at which the maximum rate of global petroleum extraction is reached. It's all downhill from there.

mid-2009 article in the *New York Times*, "over the next twenty to thirty years, vulnerable regions, particularly sub-Saharan Africa, the Middle East and South and Southeast Asia, will face the prospect of food shortages, water crises and catastrophic flooding driven by climate change that could demand an American humanitarian relief or military response."[1] And the West is next. Are you still in the mood?

Speaking of Big Os, before it gets pumped into your car, oil must be searched for, drilled, pumped, refined, and transported to your local gas station. The carbon sins continue as this nonrenewable fossil fuel spews from your engine, clogging up the atmosphere. But that's only part of the story—the entire infrastructure of modern society is based on petroleum products. Look around the room you're in right now and notice how much of your daily life revolves around plastic, one of the ubiquitous products made from oil. Then think about how the food you eat is shipped to the supermarket—or what conventional condoms are made of. Sadly, we're in a deeply abusive, codependent relationship with oil. We've created a world in which we can barely function without it, but it doesn't love us back. It's time to break the cycle and find a better energy boyfriend. (Solar and wind are fine-looking babes, by the way. Leave coal at the bar with his buddies; he's not nearly as "clean" as his lobbyist friends say he is.)

Before you drag yourself to a nunnery, consider that eco-sex can be great sex, without any loss of pleasure. This book covers important bedroom basics like eco-friendly birth-control methods, organically grown cotton and bamboo bed linens, and vegan sex toys. But it goes much farther—into all the issues that we must explore in our search for good sex. We'll look at all you do to attract a partner, from getting gussied up with organic makeup to finding vegan stilettos. You'll also learn how to woo your intended with a home-cooked meal of local, sustainable aphrodisiac foods (courtesy of celebrity chefs who know a thing or two about what to do with a cucumber). If you're in a long-term relationship that's in need of some heat, there's no need to stray or to reach for the little blue pill. Tantric sex is one of the most amazing natural alternatives to pharmaceuticals, and it's more than just fun— it's enlightening. And there are also plenty of stimulating herbs available that will make a huge, ahem, impact.

# Doin' It and Doin' It and Doin' It Well

One of the must-have books on every eco-sexual's bookshelf should be Bob Doppelt's *The Power of Sustainable Thinking*. He really lays it on the line. As a systems analyst, he understands that the propensity for quick fixes and straight-line thinking endemic to our society cannot be merged with real *sustainability*. It's just not that simple. He suggests that if we're going to do something about the environment, we've got to immerse ourselves in more holistic thinking—the same kind of idea that informs much of the alternative medicine field. If you have a serious, recurring infection under your toenail, you need

SUSTAINABILITY: The Brundtland Commission defines *sustainability* as "development that meets the needs of the present without compromising the ability of future generations to meet their own needs."[2] It's just like the Iroquois "seventh generation" philosophy, but for the rest of us.

to look at your entire immune system if you want to heal. Rubbing some balm into the affected area is not going to be a long-term solution. Similarly, recycling is a good thing to do, but it's a tiny suture to a planet-sized wound. The earth is an organism, like your body, and it needs tender, loving care at every level of its complex, intertwined system.

We're automatically attracted to that which serves our needs first; it's just the survival instinct embedded in our DNA. So we do the most convenient things, including having the most convenient sex. Doppelt calls this short-term thinking a "reactive form of cognition." *Eco-Sex* is all about understanding, examining, and getting comfortable with your instincts and recognizing how to integrate them with life as it is in the here and now. Some retrograde bits of our evolution are best left to the dustbin of history. We must embrace a new survival instinct, one that's just a bit more complicated. We're far safer in the modern world than we were when defending ourselves from the random saber-toothed tiger. The evolved eco-sexual knows where her reptilian brain ends and her natural instincts begin.

*Eco-Sex* is divided into three sections. We start with seduction in part 1 (including courtship, sexy green underthings, adornment, organic aphrodisiacs, wine, and gift giving), move on to sex and sexual health in part 2 (including condoms, the birth control pill, alternatives to Viagra, and having a healthy, sexy body), and finally explore eco-sexual adventures in part 3 (including finding fellow eco-sexuals online, green sex toys, and the green parenting movement).

# This Is How We Do It

There's a lot to love about sex. It feels great, burns calories, and stirs up megaendorphins. It's also free. Unfortunately, once you peel back the rumpled sheets of your love life, you'll uncover a messy landscape littered with potential eco-hazards, needless waste, and planet-crushing pollution. As you probably already know, sex often requires material goods, most notably birth-control devices (barrier methods) and the pill. All of these affect Mother Earth. But the bigger impact comes when your birth-control method fails—after nine months.

A die-hard eco-sexual might have his or her tubes "tied" and commit to not having kids, in order to avoid adding messy, chemical-laden birth-control by-products to the ecosystem. But that's not feasible for everyone. What everyone *can* do is think before they spawn. So let's look at this more serious side of green sex, before we move on to the fun stuff (dating, love, and everything in between).

# Sex Leads to Babies

It's the essential fact of life. And, no matter how adorable they are, babies definitely have an impact on the planet: 18 billion diapers are sold each year, and over 90 percent of them end up in landfills. And your adorable, cooing genetic replica will start driving in just about sixteen years. Unless we've figured out teleportation by that time, the impact of your child, together with everyone else's children, will be immense. Although Americans have long been the world's largest per-capita emitters of carbon dioxide, former third-world countries (India and China) are quickly catching up to us. Next time you get busy without wrapping it up, multiply your unprotected tryst by 350,000 and you'll get an idea of how many new souls are added to our planet on a daily basis.

Each year, nearly 129 million babies are born on planet Earth. That's a lot of sex. It's fantastic that so many people are having so much fun, but those who aren't seriously planning to start a family are wise to consider melting polar ice caps and rising sea levels before taking the risk. According to the British medical journal the *Lancet*, 76 million unintended pregnancies occur per year, despite the fact that women want access to contraception (sadly, over 200 million women in developing nations don't have it).[3]

But don't go blaming women in the third world for the ravages of climate change. It's Westerners, especially Americans, who use most of the world's resources. A recent study by statisticians at Oregon State University found that the *carbon footprint* of an extra child in the United States has an impact that is twenty times greater than that of environmental practices thought to make a real difference.[4] In other words, you can spend the rest of your life replacing your incandescent lightbulbs, but your efforts will be a mere drop in the bucket next to the impact of any "extra" children you have.

I'm not telling you to trash your recycling bin or give up your solar panels—just realize that your kiddies can take away your gold star for being the most eco-conscious person on the block. Think

---

CARBON FOOTPRINT: *The Dictionary of Sustainable Management* defines the term *carbon footprint* as "the total amount of greenhouse gases emitted directly and indirectly to support human activities, usually expressed in equivalent tons of either carbon or carbon dioxide."[5]

about your potential kid, and then his or her potential kid, and so on, and so on. This is about generations and generations of oxygen-swilling, carbon-emitting people. You already have a carbon legacy, and each child you produce adds 9,441 metric tons of carbon dioxide to our already hot and bothered planet.[6] At first, people might think of reducing procreation as a radical idea and worry about intrusive government and loss of personal freedom. But researchers make it clear that they're not advocating governmental controls around population issues—they're just trying to shed some light on a very real problem. So listen to them before you shed your skivvies and hop in the sack.

Swearing off children isn't the right choice for everyone and plenty of people will raise eco-conscious families that make the world a better place to live in. If you're not ready to commit to the snip, there are tons of ways to add some serious sustainability to your family life. (We'll cover this in chapter 11.)

The premise of this book is that it's not enough to do a bit of this here, a bit of that there. If you desire entry into the eco-sexual VIP room, you must change your thinking at the root level.

# Big, Fat Caveat: Health and Sustainability Are Inextricably Linked

Because the environment is so deeply intertwined with health issues, certain sections of the book will have a heavy emphasis on well-being in general. Almost everything that's bad for Mama Earth is also bad for you, and vice versa. Every suggestion made in this book is intended to wean you off of products and habits that contaminate your personal ecosystem and the ecosystem at large. Whenever we aim to reduce our consumption of industrially produced chemicals, be they in pharmaceuticals, food, clothes, sex toys, or personal care items, we're automatically making earth a safer place to live. Who will the chemical industry make *phthalates* for if no one is buying them anymore? Face it: you're not exploring eco-sexuality just because you want to save whales or trees—you're doing it to save yourself. And why wouldn't you?

The Human Toxome Project, spearheaded by the Environmental Working Group, conducted six studies of the human *body burden* and found 456 industrial pollutants, pesticides, and other chemicals in the blood, urine, and breast milk of 115 people, from newborns to teens and adults.[7] So it's going to take some major work to turn the beat around.

PHTHALATES: According to the Environmental Working Group, phthalates are "plasticizers," a group of industrial chemicals used to make plastics like polyvinyl chloride (PVC) more flexible or resilient and also as solvents. Phthalates have been found to be endocrine disruptors; they decrease sperm counts, and they cause testicular atrophy and structural abnormalities in the reproductive systems of male test animals. Some studies have linked phthalates to liver cancer, according to the U.S. Centers for Disease Control's 2005 National Report on Human Exposure to Environmental Chemicals.[8] Not sexy!

BODY BURDEN: Also known as chemical load, body burden is the amount of dangerous, toxic chemicals present in a person's body. Chemicals, both natural and human-made, find their way into the human body through inhalation, swallowing (food or liquids), and absorption through the skin.[9]

# Major Turnoffs

One fast way to deflate your libido is to consider the *life cycle assessment* (LCA), an industrial engineering buzzword. This includes everything that goes into the production of the condom that you're about to slip on or the glass of wine you're seductively pouring for someone you're hoping to lure into bed tonight. An LCA includes a lot more than raw materials, however. Think of what happened before the product got into your hot little hands: the workers in the factory where your product breathed its first breath, the energy used to power the equipment in the building, and, of course, the fuel used to ship it to the store where you purchased it. And we're not done yet: consider what happens after you toss the used product in the trash. An LCA is basically the life story of your product from cradle to grave. Every commercial product has an LCA, so an eco-sexual's first aim should be to buy items that have the least impact on the world. Your best bet, of course, is to grow your own food in your own pesticide-free soil; recycle, compost, and reuse everything you can; and tap the latex from your own personal backyard rubber tree. This is so time-consuming, however, that you may not have any energy left over for sex when you're done. If you were living on a commune and trading in the currency of free love, perhaps you could live this kind of impact-free lifestyle. But

LIFE CYCLE ASSESSMENT: According to the Environmental Protection Agency, an LCA is "a technique to assess the environmental aspects and potential impacts associated with a product, process, or service," by compiling and evaluating the energy and material inputs and environmental releases and interpreting the results to assist with informed decision-making.[10]

most of us live in cities or suburbs, and we simply can't weave our own bamboo sheets from scratch or carve a sustainable-hardwood dildo on our porch as we while away the hours. And here we get to the crux of the issue: why are you buying so much stuff in the first place? True eco-sexuals understand that we are human beings before we are consumers. The endless commodification of every facet of our lives is the real root of the ecological crisis we find ourselves in. That's why so many old-school environmentalists hate the "green" movement. They see it less as a way for people to transform the planet, and more as an opportunity for corporations to cash in on a trend. Think of it as the pleasure principle versus the profit principal. The more you tune in and turn onto eco-sexuality, the more you'll realize that your love is not for sale. Keep this less-is-more philosophy in mind as *Eco-Sex* shows you how to minimize your impact without moving to a commune (not that there's anything wrong with that).

# Greenwashing: What Advertisers Don't Want You to Know

Before we begin our adventures in eco-sex, we must talk about another very unpleasant elephant in the room: false advertising. DIY rocks and I'll explore plenty of ways to make your own creams, lotions, and massage oils in this book. However, the truth is that most of us can't always make our own lust-inducing potions, so we rely on retail products. And, try as we might, we can't always get to the health food store or order special items online, to get the most sustainably made products available. There are tons of genuine green brands emerging every day, and self-regulating companies are doing a valuable service for all of us. There are also a variety of ad hoc regulatory bodies that offer their seals of approval to truly sustainable products and can help you make better decisions as a consumer. Many virtuous, healthy and eco-conscious brands are profiled in this book. Despite that, many other companies with less savory resumes want to get in on the green "trend" and fool us into thinking that they're eco-friendly in order to get to the green in our wallets. It's absolutely vital to know what you're getting into, or putting into (or onto) yourself. The marketplace today is rife with such greenwashing, wherein companies claim that their products are green though they're clearly not. Because the United States doesn't yet have official standards in place to regulate products' environmental impact (as they do in the European Union, for instance), companies are running rampant, slapping the green imprimatur onto their products, regardless of whether they really are green.

Greenwashing takes many forms, but a common application of this practice involves emblazoning words like "natural" or "organic" on a product's label, even though the product contains an infinitesimal amount of organic ingredients. The practice is actually legal in the United States, even if the product has a hundred other dangerous chemicals, and if the single organic ingredient appears last on the list. For instance, a moisturizer with just a single drop of organic lavender oil in an otherwise toxic soup of ingredients can be advertised as a natural product. We see this magical-seeming elixir on the shelf of our local drugstore and are swept up by the earthy-looking packaging and "natural" claims—we think it's good for us. That's why it's so important to read labels, especially when you are buying products that come into close contact with your body.

Corporations won't clean up their messes until it becomes profitable for them to do so, but we can make that happen when we stop buying the crap that makes us sick. Luckily, websites like GoodGuide .com, Skin Deep (cosmeticsdatabase.com) and other *third-party certifiers* have evolved to inform us of the products that are not healthy, since our government is not yet keeping us safe from the scary slew of industrial chemicals that live in our consumer goods. By becoming informed about the dangers out there, we can spend our money on products that are truly safe and environmentally responsible, and thereby influence change in these industries.

We're aiming for what Daniel Goleman, author of *Ecological Intelligence,* calls "radical transparency," where companies openly reveal how they source the ingredients for their products, enabling us to make better, smarter choices. Because if you knew what was really in that shampoo on your local drugstore shelf, even the one screaming "organic" in big letters, you might find it decidedly unsexy.

This means consumers need to be vigilant. And vigilance isn't always compatible with sexiness. But if you do your homework in advance, you can make it seem totally effortless. Make your move, but make sure it's an eco-sexy one.

## Just the Two of Us

*Consciousness.* Wrap your brain (or your tongue) around that word for a moment. That's essentially what this book is all about. Sex is often about giving in to your intuition, listening to the needs of your

**THIRD-PARTY CERTIFIER:** Third-party certification is a scientific process by which a product, process, or service is reviewed by an unbiased, reputable third party to verify that environmental and/or health standards are being met.

body and soul. But when you add a layer of mindfulness to the heady mix of desire, pleasure, wish fulfillment, and ego boosting that is sexuality, you make the experience a whole lot richer. Eco-consciousness incorporates ethics, because reducing poverty and increasing sustainability helps all of us. It's not just about being a do-gooder and patting yourself on the back. Poverty hurts the planet, even if the poorest of the poor consume less than we do. *Fair-trade* practices encourage poor people to become sustainable consumers while also enabling them to earn a living wage that can break the generational cycle of poverty. Eco-sexuals want to create a world in which we all have enough to eat, a roof over our heads, and peace instead of war. That would be a far sexier place for all of us to live.

One of the pluses of living and loving responsibly is that it can help you attract a like-minded partner. (And there are plenty of new green dating sites that speak your language; more to come in chapter 8.) Environmental consciousness is a major turn-on in the age of climate change. Lucky for you, getting it on for the good of the planet is now possible. You can be passionate in bed *and* passionate about Mother Earth, without coming off like you're trapped on the set of the musical *Hair*. Onward, eco-sexual soldier. You're soon to be a card-carrying member of the next (and best) sexual revolution.

> FAIR TRADE: A system of trade and commerce standards in which workers are guaranteed living wages, healthy and safe working conditions, and equal employment opportunities. Designed to eradicate poverty, it empowers producers in the poorest countries in the world.[11]

PART I

# ECO-COURTSHIP: HOW TO GREEN THE DATING GAME

# chapter one

# Everything you always wanted to know about eco-regulation but were afraid to ask

Before we get to the good stuff, we've got to look at a few hard facts, ones that some might consider less than sexy. Because all things eco-friendly are very much a work in progress as of the early twenty-first century, we've got to feel our way as we go. Even the regulatory agencies and those we usually trust to tell us what's safe and healthy are blindly searching through the dark at this stage. You've got to be an eco-sleuth—an ever-vigilant, überinformed consumer—if you truly want to green your sex life. At some point there will be a global standard, but until that time comes, you can rely on all the information provided by the agencies listed here. The Web, although it can be a den of iniquity and imaginative Wikipedia entries, is also a good resource. One excellent go-to guide is Skin Deep (cosmeticsdatabase.com).

So, let's take a look at those cold, hard facts by digging deeper into greenwashing. TerraChoice Environmental Marketing (terra choice.com) has done several studies about the prevalence of greenwashing, and their 2008–2009 study revealed that greenwashing seems to be getting worse with each passing year. Here are Terra Choice's "Seven Sins of Greenwashing":[12]

**Sin of the hidden trade-off:** A claim suggesting that a product is "green" based on a narrow set of attributes without attention to other important environmental issues. Paper, for example, is not necessarily environmentally preferable just because it comes from a sustainably harvested forest. Other important environmental issues in the paper-making process, such as greenhouse gas emissions or chlorine use in bleaching, may be equally important.

**Sin of no proof:** An environmental claim that cannot be substantiated by easily accessible supporting information or by a reliable third-party certification. Common examples are facial tissues or toilet tissue products that claim various percentages of postconsumer recycled content without providing evidence.

**Sin of vagueness:** A claim that is so poorly defined or broad that its real meaning is likely to be misunderstood by the consumer. "All natural" is an example. Arsenic, uranium, mercury, and formaldehyde are all naturally occurring, and poisonous. "All natural" isn't necessarily "green."

**Sin of worshiping false labels:** A product that, through either words or images, gives the impression of third-party endorsement where no such endorsement exists—fake labels, in other words.

**Sin of irrelevance:** An environmental claim that may be truthful but is unimportant or unhelpful for consumers seeking environmentally preferable products. "CFC-free" is a common example, since it is a frequent claim despite the fact that CFCs are banned by law.

**Sin of lesser of two evils:** A claim that may be true within the product category but that risks distracting the consumer from the greater environmental impacts of the category as a whole. Organic cigarettes could be an example of this sin, as might the fuel-efficient sport-utility vehicle.

**Sin of fibbing:** Environmental claims that are simply false. The most common examples were products falsely claiming to be Energy Star certified or registered.

# Living in Sin

The SIN (Substitute It Now!) list was developed by the European Union (in concert with nongovernmental organizations, or NGOs) in 2008. The list consists of 267 chemicals that are identified as "Substances of Very High Concern." We have no similar system in place in the United States yet, so we must rely on our wits (and Internet searching skills). According to Skin Deep (cosmeticsdatabase.com), "90 percent of ingredients used in personal care products have not been evaluated for safety by any publicly accountable institution. And as people apply an average of 126 unique ingredients on their skin daily, these chemicals are raising concerns, for their potential impacts to human health and to the environment."[13]

## The Top Fifteen Toxic Ingredients to Avoid in Personal Care Products

This list is by no means comprehensive, but it provides a good cheat sheet to rely on when you're perusing the drugstore or supermarket shelves and want to avoid the most deadly ingredients.

1. **Synthetic fragrances:** Unless the label says it's derived from essential oils, avoid anything that says "fragrance." These almost always contain the ever-evil phthalates, poisonous chemicals that will eventually be phased out. For now, avoid them.

2. **Parabens:** Even though the word is pretty much out on the dangers of these preservatives, a lot of companies still haven't gotten the memo. Or they have gotten the memo but ignored it because they care more about their bottom line than about your body. Avoid at all costs.

3. **Ureas:** These contain formaldehyde. On labels they will be described as diazolidinyl urea, imidazolidinyl urea, or DMDM hydantoin. These can cause contact dermatitis. Yuck.

4. **1, 4-dioxane:** This is a chemical carcinogen derived from petroleum. Don't go there.

5. **Chemical sunscreens:** They came, they saw, they disrupted your endocrine system. Avoid oxybenzone and octylmethoxy-cinnamate like the plague.

6. **Amines:** Ammonia compounds are used as foaming agents. Use these if you're a masochist and would like a nice, painful allergic reaction and eye irritation to go with your cleansing routine. They are listed as MEA, DEA, and TEA on ingredients labels.

7. **Sulfates:** You've probably heard of these by now, since even the commercial manufacturers are removing them from their hair-care products. Why? Because the public shouted, loud, about how horrible they are. Sodium lauryl and sodium laureth sulfate should be thought of as the two evil stepsisters of shampoo. Run the other way screaming.

8. **Petrochemicals:** Talk about crude. Derived from petroleum, these nasties are better known as petrolatum, mineral oil, and paraffin. It sucks that they're made from oil sources, but it's even more gross that they clog your pores and give you zits galore.

9. **Synthetic colors:** FD&C or D&C followed by a color and number on a label indicates a synthetic color. They contain coal tar and are full of heavy metals that irritate the skin. And guess what? They're carcinogenic. Yes, these were in the food coloring that you used to dye eggs and any pink or purple cupcakes you ate as a child. Oh, joy.

10. **Synthetic polymers:** Carbomer and sodium polyacrylate make products gooey, but they also come from petroleum, so move on.

11. **Antibacterials:** Chlorphenesin and triclosan are icky mainly because they go down the drain and into the waterways. Along with our overuse of prescribed antibiotics, this practice may create resistant strains of terrible diseases like H1N1, SARS, and scary superbugs.

12. **Chelators:** Disodium EDTA and tetrasodium EDTA can form nitrosamines. You don't need to know what that means, but you do need to know that they're carcinogens. Put that product back on the shelf, baby.

13. **Toluene:** Can you guess what's in your nail polish? Yes, it's toluene, which is also used in gasoline as a binding agent.

14. **Talc:** You thought that baby powder was innocent, but it's not.

15. **Propylene glycol:** This stuff is everywhere. Used in antifreeze, as a deicer, and in latex, paint, and laundry detergent, this evil ingredient causes irritation of nasal and respiratory passages

and, if you're dumb enough to eat it, can cause nausea, vomiting, and diarrhea.

And finally, the bonus ingredient: nanoparticles. What's terrifying about them is that they're so new and so potentially hazardous that we have no clue what they do, how they do it, and why. They are totally unregulated, and environmental experts warn they will be used in many products. They may sound all cool and *Star Trek*, but avoid them until scientists have more time to properly vet them.

# Creating Boundaries: The Governments, Organizations and Websites on Your Side

Because the world of eco-friendly products is still a bit like the Wild West, we need smart people to tell us what's safe, clean, and green. Here's a list of organizations that exist to give us a semblance of knowledge and reassurance about what is safe to put on, in, or near our bodies.

## North America

**USDA National Organic Program** (ams.usda.gov/nop) is a government agency that oversees national organic standards and accredits organic certification agencies. Of the hundred or so certifying agencies that use USDA standards to certify products, about half are domestic. The other half certify overseas products to standards set by the USDA.

**California Certified Organic Farmers**, or CCOF (ccof.org), uses USDA organic and CCOF international standards to certify not only farmers, but also processors, restaurants, and retailers.

**Fair Trade** (fairtrade.net), known as "fair-trade certified" in the United States and Canada, allows consumers to choose products that not only meet environmental standards, but also those concerning labor and the development of community resources.

**The Compact for Safe Cosmetics** (safecosmetics.org) is a pledge that companies sign as part of the Campaign for Safe Cosmetics. The European Union standards on the use of chemicals that cause or are believed to cause cancer, birth defects, and mutations are strong, and the compact's pledge requires companies to meet or exceed those standards.

**Greenseal** (greenseal.org) is an independent, nonprofit organization that uses science-based standards to encourage the marketplace to create a greener world.

**The Leaping Bunny Program** (leapingbunny.org) of the Coalition for Consumer Information on Cosmetics (CCIC) allows companies to use their logo if their cosmetics and household products are deemed cruelty-free. When you see the cute little bunny logo, you are assured that no animal testing was involved in the production, whether by the company or its suppliers.

**People for the Ethical Treatment of Animals** (peta.org) use their PETA symbol to offer assurance that products have not been tested on animals. PETA is the organization that brought us the sexy "I'd rather go naked than wear fur" ads.

**The Scientific Certification Systems Greenhouse Gas Verification Program** (scscertified.com) provides third-party verification for forestry and land-use projects that seek to provide climate benefits by reducing greenhouse gas emissions. They claim that their independent verification services ensure that emissions reductions claims are credible, transparent, and tradable in international carbon markets.

**The Forest Stewardship Council**, or FSC (fsc.org) is an independent, nonprofit organization that is not associated with any government. It is international, and sets high standards for the use of forests.

**ISO** (iso.org) is the International Organization for Standardization. Companies that use this seal may have progressive labor and environmental practices. Check the specific regulation number mentioned on the ISO seal to see which practices the product is certified for.

**Green America** (greenamericatoday.org), formerly Co-op America, is an organization that approves businesses that use business as a tool for positive social change by being values driven as well as profit driven. Such businesses responsibly source, manufacture, and market their products and employ practices that benefit workers, communities, customers, and the environment.[14]

**The Canadian Organic Standard** (ota.com/pp/canada.html) requires that products calling themselves organic on the front label must have at least 95 percent organic ingredients. If less than 70 percent of its ingredients are organic, it can only list the organic ingredients, and can't call itself an organic product overall.

## Europe

**European Standards** (ec.europa.eu/agriculture/organic/home_en) for organic products are similar to the USDA standards. The EU organic farming logo is the seal required, as of July 2010, on all organic products sold in the EU. The one big difference between the European standards and USDA standards is that products with less than 70 percent organic ingredients may not be labeled with the word *organic* at all under EU regulations, while in the United States companies are allowed to indicate which specific ingredients are organic.

**The Soil Association** (soilassociation.org) in the United Kingdom is an example of a certifying body with stricter requirements than those of the government regulations.

**BDIH** (kontrollierte-naturkosmetik.de/e/bdih.htm) certification is a German agency that surpasses national and EU standards.

**ECOCERT** (ecocert.com) certifies foods to national organic standards (USDA, JAS, EU), but for cosmetics some feel that its standards are quite lax. Better than nothing, however!

## Asia

**The Japanese Agriculture Standard** (imo.ch/imo_services_organic_jas_standard_en.html) certifies organic products that carry a special seal. When organic products enter the United States from Japan, it is the MAFF/USDA Export Arrangement that governs the decision whether those products will get the USDA organic seal.

## Oceania

**The Australian Organic Standard** (daff.gov.au/aqis/export/organic-bio-dynamic) requires that, for products labeled organic, all of the ingredients, with the exception of salt and water, must be derived from organic production methods. Tough standards, to be sure, but that's one good reason to trust the Aussies when it comes to green.

**New Zealand's Official Organic Assurance Program**, or OOAP (nzfsa.govt.nz/organic), has strict standards, much like those of the Australians. What's in the water over in Oceania? We need some of that in the United States.

## International

**Demeter International** (demeter.net) is a certification program whose label can only be applied to products made with ingredients grown using biodynamic agriculture. No one can use the brand unless they are under a legal and tightly controlled contract with Demeter. Demeter's requirements generally exceed government-mandated regulations.

**IFOAM** (ifoam.org) certification is given by the International Organic Accreditation Service (IOAS), which seeks to provide an overarching seal of approval that meets organic standards internationally, not just according to one nation's standards.

# Seeing Through You:
# The Art of Transparency

Daniel Goleman, author of *Ecological Intelligence*, imagines a world in which transparency rules the marketplace. During the summer of 2009 Walmart, in association with several universities, introduced its "Sustainability Consortium," which will purportedly measure the LCAs of all products and post a single rating next to each product on the shelves. If Walmart continues to use mainly unregulated Chinese suppliers for the bulk of its goods, it will probably be hard for eco-advocates to give the consortium a stamp of approval, no matter how transparent Walmart's practices become. In addition, Monsanto, Cargill, and Unilver, three major corporations with bad environmental track records, are listed on the website (sustainability consortium.org) as founders of the project.

With these red flags, it's too early to tell whether this is green or greenwash. As this book goes to press, the consortium is in its infancy and will take at least five years to roll out. Walmart has a history of supporting bad labor practices, and if they want to set the standard for what's truly good for the earth, they'll need to ensure fairness for their workers, among other things. We'll see how it all plays out.

Now that you know what to avoid, it's time to get your gorgeous on.

# CHAPTER TWO

# ECO-gorgeousness: MUCH MORE THAN SKIN DEEP

Beauty rituals, ancient and modern, have long been used to lure lovers. When we feel beautiful, we radiate confidence and sexiness, and no hot-blooded creature can resist that. How dreadful, however, that the very stuff we rely on to make us gorgeous can also make us sick. Just as you want to avoid polluting the earth, you want to avoid polluting the ecosystem that is your body.

The cosmetics industry is notorious for mixing together chemical brews that do far more damage than good. A ridiculously expensive wrinkle cream that claims to prevent aging may temporarily plump up the skin on your forehead, but you don't want to know what it's doing to your insides. Everything you put on your skin goes directly into the systems of your body—you might as well be eating that jar of La Mer for dessert.

Similarly, sexy, mass-produced fashions may look great, but they can harm the earth and lower the quality of life for workers in developing nations. If you knew that low-cut dress was made from petroleum-derived fibers woven by children forced into labor in Indonesia, would you feel as smokin' hot sashaying down the street? It might show off your cleavage, but it's also showing off your apathy, and that ain't sexy.

# Nothing's Sexier (or Has a Smaller Carbon Footprint) than Self-Esteem

Statistics show that millions of women are unsatisfied with their sex lives. If you're too busy thinking about the size of your thighs, your pores, your acne or wrinkles, or what have you, how can you possibly relax enough to feel comfortable naked? Even in the act of sex many women don't let themselves go because they're busy wondering if their partner has noticed their imagined flaws. Sex is about getting lost in the moment. You can't get lost while obsessing on what your partner thinks about your body (or even your technique).

Men in heterosexual relationships often underestimate how much time and energy their partners spend on beauty, and how much this contributes to mutual sexual satisfaction. Women feel better when they feel attractive. In an ideal world it wouldn't matter, and feminists are quite right when they show us how the "beauty myth" has wrecked our collective sense of self. (Thank you, Naomi Wolf.) But the truth is that we live in this world and we must work with the tools we have in the here and now, not the ones that twenty years of intensive psychotherapy and the outlawing of supermodels might give us. So even if you're an ultraprogressive vegan, radical anarchist, and green warrior, you shouldn't feel bad about wanting to be pretty. It's only when we become sick and obsessive about perfection that our sex lives (and the other parts of our lives) begin to wither away and die. In fact, eco-sexuals can create a new standard, one in which feminists and unrepentant divas can compare notes and agree to disagree about the height of their respective heels and ideals. This book aims to hit that sweet spot between feeling naturally, wildly attractive and having a mind-blowing sex life. Even if you're one of the lucky women who loves her bod without working at it, you'll enjoy dabbling in the lovely beautification rituals in this chapter. This is about feeling attractive as a human being, not as an idealized, airbrushed woman.

Fortunately, we no longer have to give up an ounce of beauty and chicness in pursuit of eco-consciousness. Although a lot of big, bad corporations continue to hide their production methods from buyers, more and more manufacturers are moving toward radical transparency. Some who've been in the biz forever are changing their processes, and others have started new companies based on eco-friendly principles. Still, it can be tough to identify those that are truly green.

## The Many Nuances of Green

In the personal care products category, there are many companies that are on the green bandwagon purely for the marketing cachet. Others are doing it because they're true believers who want to make the world a better place. Somewhere in the middle are those who wouldn't necessarily call themselves green but have healthy formulations that will not harm your body's ecosystem or the ecosystem at large. This is one of the sticky wickets of the environmental movement's relationship with consumer goods. For the purposes of this book, especially when it comes to beauty products, I've included companies that may not seem all that green at first glance. They may not be running down the street screaming, "Look at me! I'm green!" but they are greening the world in subtle but important ways.

Nevertheless, greenwashing is rampant, and often the companies with the biggest marketing budgets, flashiest packaging, and most flawless press releases are the very ones that are lying to you. Read between the lines.

The Campaign for Safe Cosmetics (safecosmetics.org) is a great place to start searching for pure products. Their Compact for Safe Cosmetics has emerged to fill in some of the gaps in government regulation. According to safecosmetics.org, the companies that sign on to the compact agree to the following:[15]

*Provision 1: Comply with the EU Cosmetics Directive ingredient prohibitions and ingredient nomenclature standards in all markets.*

The European Union bans more than 1,100 toxic ingredients, including chemicals linked to cancer and birth defects, from personal care products; the U.S. Food and Drug Administration bans only 11. [You do the math.]

*Provision 2: Disclose all ingredients.*

One of the most important concepts of the Compact for Safe Cosmetics is transparency and public accountability. By signing the compact, companies agree to post a full list of their product ingredients on their company website and in the Skin Deep database so that consumers can know what's in the products they're using. Toxic chemicals can sometimes hide in ingredient listings; for example, hazardous chemicals like phthalates are a common component of the ingredient "fragrance."

*Provision 3: Publish and regularly update product information in EWG's Skin Deep database.*

Companies are required to update their product information at least once a year.

But why should we bother? Because beauty is much more than skin deep—it's cell deep. Many of the chemicals in personal care products don't get flushed out of our bodies—they can linger for years in our organs, and it's nearly impossible to detox from them,

*Provision 4: Comply with ingredient prohibitions and restrictions under the Compact for Safe Cosmetics and substitute ingredients of concern with safer alternatives.*

Signers must develop a plan that prioritizes ingredients with known health concerns for substitution—and implement solutions—within three years of signing the compact.

*Provision 5: Substantiate the safety of all products and/or ingredients with publicly available data.*

Without adequate toxicity data, there is no way to assess whether an ingredient is safe or not. Currently only 11 percent of the ingredients used in cosmetics have ever been tested for safety. The Compact for Safe Cosmetics asks that before a product is put on the market, reasonable proof of no harm should be established by consulting peer-reviewed scientific publications and publicly available industry studies. Companies are required to submit assessments, the best of which are peer-reviewed studies that consider the impact of cumulative exposure and repeated use, and that recognize exposures to vulnerable populations such as infants and pregnant women.

*Provision 6: Participate in the Campaign for Safe Cosmetics.*

Companies must actively participate in the Campaign by attending meetings or conference calls, providing product data, and submitting annual signed certification of compliance with the compact.

especially if you continue to use them every day. Parabens, used as a preservative for decades, are particularly scary. They have found their way into almost every personal care item, including shampoos, moisturizers, and cleansers. The EPA has found that parabens mimic estrogenic activity and can disrupt the endocrine system. This can in turn alter a whole host of systems within your body, wreaking havoc with the hypothalamus, thyroid, and ovaries. It can disrupt menstrual cycles, which can cause fertility issues, breast cancer, and weight gain. And if you're a guy, well, you really don't want all that extra estrogen unless you're actively initiating a sex change (not that there's anything wrong with that).

This is one of the many reasons that truly organic alternatives are so necessary. But an exhaustive search for chemical-free, consciously produced cosmetics and skin-care products may seem daunting, especially since the FDA isn't helping in this area yet. Fortunately, there is

## Ready, Set: Date Prep

Getting ready for a hot night with a new or potential lover can be just as fun as the date itself. Well, maybe not just as fun, but anticipation is a heady aphrodisiac. Eco-sex is all about indulging in sensuality. If you make the hours before a date into a thoughtful and playful ritual, you'll be far more relaxed and open on your date. This book has assembled everything a DIY eco-sexual could possibly need for her romantic adventures. Set the mood for your predate solo time— light soy candles, play your favorite music, and make it your intention to have the best night of your life. Imagining yourself a modern-day Cleopatra or Aphrodite can do wonders for your mood, and you don't have to reveal your secrets—all he'll see is your ethereal glow.

a way to avoid spending all your time and energy trying to find the good stuff. Consult the Campaign for Safe Cosmetics website or look for some of the organizations and certifications listed in the previous chapter. Once you get the hang of identifying companies that green-wash, you'll easily find your way to those with integrity and high green standards.

# DIY Beauty

Store-bought green products are necessary for the time-crunched among us. But if you're blessed with a little bit of leisure time before your date, why not go DIY? The lovely Janice Cox, coauthor of *EcoBeauty*, has generously shared some of her favorite recipes with us. The best part about them is that you won't need to shop for fancy ingredients—you probably already have most of them in your cupboard or fridge.

## A Facial Mask for All Skin Types (and for All Seasons)

*A good facial mask softens the skin, unclogs the pores, and removes any surface impurities. It also helps replace lost moisture and soothe the skin, helping your complexion to look healthy and radiant. This is a recipe for a basic facial mask that can be used by all skin types. Because you are making it at home, you can easily adjust the ingredients to meet your skin's needs. Try to use all-organic ingredients when possible. Fresh fruit masks are a great way to use up really ripe fruits, which are softer for mashing anyway!*

$^1/_2$ cup sour cream or plain yogurt
1 teaspoon honey

For oily skin types, add 1 egg white and $^1/_4$ cup grated fresh apple
For dry skin types, add 1 egg yolk and $^1/_2$ ripe banana, mashed
For acne-prone skin types, add $^1/_2$ cup mashed fresh strawberries

Mix all the ingredients together into a smooth paste (a spoon or the back of a fork works well, but a blender will produce the smoothest mask). Spread on your face and leave on for 15 minutes. Rinse your face clean with warm water and pat your skin dry. Follow with your favorite moisturizer.

Yield: 4 to 6 ounces

# Brown Sugar Body Scrub

*For super smooth and sexy skin, you cannot beat an all-over sugar scrub. Sugar is perfect for all skin types because it is gentle and mild and won't irritate your skin. A natural humectant, sugar attracts and holds moisture. Apply this scrub all over your body (avoiding the nether regions) before bathing. You may also want to add a bit of vanilla extract for scent— vanilla is a well-known aphrodisiac enjoyed by both men and women.*

1 cup dark brown sugar
$^1/_4$ cup almond oil
$^1/_2$ teaspoon vitamin E oil
$^1/_2$ teaspoon vanilla extract (optional)

In a bowl, stir together all the ingredients until well blended. Spoon into a clean jar with a tight-fitting lid. To use, while standing in the tub or shower, massage 1 or 2 tablespoons of the scrub all over your body to gently exfoliate and moisturize your skin. Rinse well and follow with a rich natural oil or moisturizer.

Yield: 10 ounces

## Amorous Bath Oil

*Roses, the classic symbol of love and beauty, are almost cliché. But that doesn't make their scent any less divine, calming, and relaxing. This bath oil combination is the perfect preparation for a romantic date or part of a special evening together. For bulk organic roses and rose petals, try FiftyFlowers.com.*

1 cup rose water
2 tablespoons light sesame oil
1 teaspoon vitamin E oil
5 or 6 drops essential oil of roses
Fresh rose petals

In a small bowl, stir together the rose water, sesame oil, vitamin E oil, and essential oil, then pour into a clean bottle or container. To use, shake the closed container gently to combine, then pour under the running water while filling your bathtub. Scatter fresh rose petals into the bath and indulge.

Yield: 8 ounces, enough for 1 bath

# Green Goods from the Store or Online

What if you're pressed for time and would rather buy your decadent goodies at the store or online? There are tons of high-quality options available to you, especially if you go for multipurpose products. The beauty industry has convinced you that you need separate products to cleanse your face and body, and that you need to stick with one line for all your beauty needs. It's pure bunk—they just want you to buy more of their stuff. Another tip? Beware companies that suggest you use generous portions (the old "lather, rinse, and repeat" routine). Instead, stick to brands that do more with less product, so you spend less and dispose of packaging less often. Sustainable NYC is a brick-and-mortar business for locals in New York City with a lovely array of personal care products. Lucky for you, they also sell online at sustainable-nyc.com.

## Scrubs

### Body

For the body, you might try Trillium Organics, which makes a fantastic line of scrubs, oils, soaps, perfumes, and more. The company's Organic Body Polish is a skin-smoothing dream, especially the warming Clementine Clove variety. Be careful when exfoliating—avoid broken skin or rashy areas.

### Face

When exfoliating the face, be gentle, darling, gentle. We've been over-scrubbing our delicate facial tissue for years, rampantly using alpha hydroxy acids (AHAs) in the interest of abating wrinkles and zits alike. There are better ways to address these problems, namely ridding your body of toxic substances. In the meantime, try Farmaesthetics Sweet Milk & Lavender Exfoliant (not for vegans, however). Pangea Organics Egyptian Geranium with Adzuki Bean & Cranberry Facial Scrub is safe for vegans, smells divine, and works brilliantly.

## Bath Oils

What a lovely way to get in the mood. Dr. Hauschka Rose Bath Oil, Inara Babassu Milk Bath, and Erbaviva Embrace Bath Oil are all sensuous, green, and stimulating to body and mind.

## Cleansers for Face and Body

Farmaesthetics Fine Herbal Cleanser is light and lovely smelling, and it works with the scrub mentioned above. Best of all, it's dual purpose—you can use it on your face and body.

## Hair Products

John Masters's brilliant line of products for hair is a green miracle. This is one of the rare lines in which genuine eco-consciousness, health, and purity meet with quality. People often say that shampoos are among the hardest products to get right when a line is trying to go green. Hair products are some of the worst eco-offenders, creating chemical brews that rival Three Mile Island. Sulfides are extremely toxic and dangerous, and they are the first ingredient on most conventional shampoos, but they don't have to be. Mr. Masters's Rosemary Shampoo proves that you don't have to douse yourself with chemicals in order to leave your shower with great-looking hair. His Deep Scalp Follicle Treatment & Volumizer works wonders on a scalp that's been victimized by scary products for years. Other winning brands in this category include Intelligent Nutrients and Living Nature. No time to wash your hair? Try Lulu Organics Organic Hair Powder. Just shake it through and go.

The moral here is that you can heal from all those years of blow-drying, coloring, perming, and styling—if you lay off the sauce and start using stuff that's good for you.

## Hair Removal Products

Disposable razors are a landfill's nightmare. They're made of plastic, and you already know that petroleum products are bringing us quickly to our demise. Preserve Razors have handles made from recycled plastic (65 percent from Stonyfield Farm yogurt cups).

If you dare to tear your body hair at the root by waxing, try Moom, which uses 100 percent certified organic wax and essential oil blends in its formulas. It doesn't take the ouch out, but it definitely takes the toxins out.

## Masks

Pangea Organics's all-purpose mask is made with Japanese matcha tea, açai, and goji berry, but that doesn't tell you why it's so damn good. It works for acneic skin, aging skin, and all the skin in between. It clarifies and tones, stimulates collagen production, and detoxifies clogged skin. Even better, Pangea has real green street cred. All products are hand blended in small batches, and most ingredients are organic or purchased through fair trade. Joshua Scott Onysko, founder and CEO of Pangea Organics, is in the process of creating a foundation to support better business practices.

## Toners

Here's a secret that the beauty industry doesn't want you to know: you don't have to tone, especially if you're over thirty and your skin is on the dry side. You need nothing more than witch hazel to get that tight Bonne Bell feeling you may still be addicted to. If you simply must have a store-bought product, go for Dr. Alkaitis's Organic Herbal Toner or Simply Divine's Gypsy Rose Tea.

## Moisturizers

Nothing is sexier than a soft, dewy complexion. Go forth and moisturize.

### Face

Wanna go super simple? Cleanse and moisturize your face and/or body with pure coconut oil. Although this might sound a bit icky at first—after all, you cook with it—it's a wonderful multipurpose oil. Amazingly, it doesn't clog pores, and because it's a natural antibacterial substance, it will help heal your skin. You can even use it as an eye makeup remover, and it will condition your eyelashes in the process. This is excellent for mature skin or any skin on the dry side of the spectrum, but works well even for oily types. Virgin Oil de Coco-Créme by Quality First International is a non-GMO, certified organic, cold-pressed, vitamin E–rich product that you can use internally and externally (it's great for cooking and awesome in smoothies). You can buy it from oneluckyduck.com.

Another excellent option in this category is argan oil, made from the *Argania spinosa* tree, which grows only in Morocco and can live up to two hundred years. A Berber women's cooperative produces the oil, and Shea Terra's argan is certified by Ecocert, although it's not fair-trade certified. You only need one or two drops for the face. It's also a great body moisturizer, is soothing on the décolleté, and works as a hair oil. Remember, just as truth is beauty, multipurpose is green.

If you're not into any of the multipurpose possibilities listed above try anything from Simply Divine's line, where you'll find a crème for every concern.

## Body

It's so hard to pick just one product in the body moisturizers category. Lots of brands are making absolutely delicious creams, oils, and lotions that your skin will fall madly in love with. Simply Divine Botanicals is a mostly organic, handcrafted line; the How Now Brown

## Greening Your Pearly Whites

You're naked without your smile, so treat your mouth, gums, and teeth to some grand ol' greening.

BRUSHING: Forget the fluoride, eco-warriors—it's thought to cause cancer. DIY your toothpaste instead. Plain old baking soda works to clean your teeth in a delightful way. You can also mix it with hydrogen peroxide. Salt is also excellent for cleaning the mouth and gums. If you long for a minty kick, add some peppermint oil. If you're an anti-DIY diva, try any of the products from Eco-Dent (eco-dent.com)— they also have awesome floss.

BRIGHTENING: Store-bought teeth whiteners are full of chemicals, not to mention waste (trays, packaging, and the works). But the

Cacao is a liquid chocolate bar in a jar that melts into your skin like butter. The cocoa smell lasts for hours, so just make sure you're not around any bees (except for the metaphorical ones that hang out with birds). Exceptionally sensual and totally beautifying, Dr. Hauschka's Rose Body Oil is another standby. Be careful not to run late for your date because you're having too much fun in the bathroom with the nice German doctor.

## Eyes and Lips
RMS Lip and Skin Balm is a great under-eye moisturizer that also works for lips. Weleda's light, nonirritating Intensive Wild Rose eye cream soaks into the delicate under-eye area and can be used on the lids as well. It's perfect under makeup or on its own. And Weleda's lip balm is to die for.

humble strawberry is your secret brightening weapon. An organic strawberry and baking soda are all you need. Crush the strawberry to a pulp (the malic acid makes it work) and mash it up with a $^1/_2$ teaspoon of baking soda. You can rub it onto your teeth with your fingers or a toothbrush. Leave it on for five minutes and voilà!—instant, natural whitening. Just make sure not to do it too often (no more than once a week) as the malic acid can damage tooth enamel.

EVERY BREATH YOU TAKE: Your garden (or the health food store) can yield some great breath fresheners. Coriander, anise, clove, or fresh mint will sweeten up your kisses. Or chew on a cinnamon stick. A sip of liquid chlorophyll in the morning soothes your digestion, which automatically deodorizes your mouth.

*Feet*

Revolution Organics's USDA Certified Organic All-Over Body Balm comes in stick form and is filled with food-grade ingredients. Use it on your feet or anywhere else—for fly-aways, on the lips, even to prime skin for makeup.

## Cellulite

Cellulite is a bitch, ladies. But Weleda's Birch Cellulite Oil is, in two words, the bomb. It has a lovely, light scent, not like some of the more medicinal ones in this category. The most important thing is, it really does seem to work on skin dimples, although it contains no harsh chemicals or caffeine, a common ingredient in cellulite creams. The trick is to keep your skin slightly damp from your shower and spend a few minutes rubbing it in. Your thighs will thank you.

## Nail Polishes

Peacekeeper Cause-metics nail polish was rated by the Environmental Working Group as the safest paint-based natural nail polish. And they have really sexy colors.

## Makeup

It's RMS Beauty (rmsbeauty.com) all the way, baby. You don't need anything but these totally pure products for lips, eyes, cheeks, and foundation. Working as a celebrity makeup artist for more than twenty years, Rose-Marie Swift became sick from absorbing all the poisonous chemicals in cosmetics. After finding out that she had toxic loads of aluminum, mercury, cadmium, barium, and lead, as well as pesticides and other solvents, in her body, she made it her mission to create a brand that would make women beautiful without killing them slowly. After years of testing, fearlessly fighting for chemical-free formulas, and going from lab to lab to find one that would live up to her standards, she unveiled RMS Beauty in 2008. It may be the only cosmetics line that is almost 100 percent organic. There is nothing out there with the street cred of this line—it's the real deal when it comes to health for your body and health for the earth. RMS is a Compact for Safe Cosmetics signer, which is always a good thing.

RMS's "Un" Cover-Up is a moisturizing concealer that lends a healthy glow and blends with your skin tone. The truly awesome part is that you can also use it as a foundation. You don't need both a concealer stick and a separate bottle of foundation anymore—just dip into her recyclable glass jars and dab a bit more thickly in the areas that need assistance. Even if you were out last night until the wee hours, this product will make it look like you got thirteen hours of sleep. It also covers any red spots without clogging pores. Rose-Marie calls her makeup "finger food" because you don't need brushes, just your digits. Even better, you don't need to worry about chemical preservatives or icky bacteria invading the jars. The base of all her products is organic coconut oil, a naturally antimicrobial substance. It's pretty much a magical elixir that will change your life forever. Add a bit of her Living Luminizer anywhere you'd like a bit of glow without the tacky glitter you get with other products.

Women of color will love the USDA-certified organic mineral makeup from Afterglow Cosmetics, free of bismuth oxychloride, a common toxin found in many mineral makeup brands. Afterglow makes products for your face, eyes, and lips. Their sustainable, socially responsible ethos is pretty gorgeous, too.

## Eye Shadow

Sorry to be a broken record, but there's nothing out there like RMS in this category. Every color is absolutely beautiful, and a little goes a long way because it's very deeply pigmented. RMS shadows give you the endlessly sexy "wet look" that's been so popular on fashion runways in recent years. Magnetic, a best seller, is a great go-to color to give the lids a sexy, natural shimmer if you use a light touch. The more you use, the deeper the color on your skin. A lot of the shadow colors also work for lips and cheeks.

## Mascara

It's hard to find a truly green mascara, but Dr. Hauschka's is lovely, nonirritating, and only comes off if you cry. And you won't be crying on your hot date, I hope.

## Eyeliner

Check out Cargo's PlantLove liners. They come in an excellent array of colors, have real staying power, and won't harm your sensitive peepers.

## Lips

In 2007 the Campaign for Safe Cosmetics released a report entitled "A Poison Kiss: The Problem of Lead in Lipstick".[16] Although California legislators tried to pass a law to regulate the occurrence of this dangerous substance in lipsticks, it was stopped by lobbyists. Luckily, alternatives exist—you don't have to live with a naked pout in order to avoid permanent brain damage. Lavera is a BDIH-certified makeup and skin-care line that makes some absolutely gorgeous and healthy lipsticks.

# Scent and Sensibility

Synthetic perfumes are a minefield. No one likes being in a closed room with a clueless person who has unknowingly applied too much Chanel No. 5. The sneezing, choking, headaches, and burning sensations in the throat one gets in such situations aren't that surprising, given the ingredients in perfumes. The masterful work of marketers over many decades has made this industry into one with a magical cachet—and one that does a superb job of hiding what's really in those products: 80 to 90 percent of fragrances are petroleum derived. The chemicals in perfume are volatile organic compounds (VOCs)— the very chemicals we try to avoid in paint and other household products. We spray them into the air, inhaling them into our lungs, and we put them on our pulse points where they are absorbed into the skin. Perfumers are known for using "proprietary blends," which essentially means they don't have to tell the FDA if they're using poison in their formulas. There is virtually no regulation at all in this arena.

Some of these blends have been reported to cause breast cells to produce estrogen in excessive amounts. Looking for a cosmetically induced lobotomy? Neurotoxins have a causal link to central nervous system disorders, allergic reactions, dizziness, tinnitus, skin and eye irritations, double vision, sneezing, nasal congestion, sinusitis, ear pain, vertigo, anaphylaxis, coughing, bronchitis, breathing and swallowing difficulty, headaches, seizures, fatigue, confusion, disorientation, short-term memory loss, impaired concentration, nausea, lethargy, anxiety, irritability, depression, mood swings, restlessness, rashes, hives, eczema, facial flushing, muscle and joint pain, irregular heartbeat, hypertension, swollen lymph glands, and more. The myriad health problems blamed on secondhand perfume exposure are causing owners of some public buildings to adopt policies banning perfumes, with good reason.

People have used aromatics for beauty, therapeutic, medicinal, and ritual uses for thousands of years. Only in the last hundred or so years did we begin using synthetic scents, which get under our skin and into our nasal cavities.

Persephenie, a Los Angeles–based priestess of aromatherapy (persephenie.com) says scent directly stimulates our senses with its ability to spark attraction, warning, memories, recognition, and communication. The term *aromatherapy* was first used by the French chemist and perfumer René-Maurice Gattefossé. Aromatherapy affects our senses by activating physiological and emotional responses. When scent enters the nasal cavity, it immediately travels to the limbic system, the area of our brain where memory is retained and where emotion is recognized. The limbic system then sends a signal, based on which aroma is sensed, to the hypothalamus, the brain's center for basic drives and emotions. Next, the hypothalamus trig-

## Love Stinks

Why do you sometimes swoon when you smell your lover's armpit? (Go on, admit it.) Although the scientific jury is still out on how it works in humans, some studies have shown that odor cues connected to the immune system help us to select mates who aren't closely related to us (you know, to keep you from sleeping with your brother). The word *pheromone* translates to "transferred excitement."

gers the pituitary gland to emit various hormones, which affect the entire body.

Aromas clearly have an overwhelming effect on the body—but when they're synthetic, it's deadly, not sexy. To avoid inhaling and absorbing dangerous substances, why not make your own healthy, heady, and potent DIY scents?

## DIY Alternatives to Deadly Synthetic Fragrances

Thinking about trying DIY natural perfume? You'll need the following to make Persephenie's stellar scents:

+ Base oil, such as organic almond, jojoba, grape seed, or coconut oil

+ Glass droppers

+ Bottles to contain the blended mixes

+ Rubbing alcohol to help clean essential oils off glass and ceramics

The following are three simple scent recipes from Persephenie's private vault. Dab them on your pulse points, and don't forget behind the ear and the knee. For each of the formulas below, use 15 to 25 drops of essential oil per ounce of base oil. (Use less essential oil for children, pregnant women, or anyone in weak health.)

# Scent to Seduce a Man

*Wear this blend to seduce that hunky man you've had your eye on.*

15 drops rose geranium essential oil
6 drops rose absolute essential oil
3 drops vanilla essential oil
1 ounce (2 tablespoons) base oil

# Scent to Seduce a Woman

*Wear this blend to attract that lovely lady you've been pining after.*

18 drops cedarwood essential oil
3 drops vetiver essential oil
3 drops vanilla essential oil
1 ounce (2 tablespoons) base oil

# Libido-Stimulating Scent

*This can be used by either sex and also works beautifully in a soy-based wax candle, should you and your honey decide to do some arts and crafts as foreplay. (Candle making is a rather involved process, so make sure you know what you're doing before you give it a try.)*

18 drops cedarwood essential oil
6 drops patchouli essential oil
3 drops ginger essential oil
1 1/2 ounces (3 tablespoons) base oil

# Aphrodisiac Essential Oil Profiles

Try a dab of this or a smidgen of that depending on your mood and what you're hoping to attract.

*Ambrette (Abelmoschus moschatus)*
A stimulating yet narcotically calming musky, floral known for its exotic aphrodisiac scent, ambrette is extracted from the seed of *Abelmoschus moschatus* and is a botanical alternative to the glandular secretions of the musk deer. But this way, Bambi doesn't have to die for your sex life.

*Cedarwood (Cedrus deodara)*
Symbolic for strength, endurance, and certainty, cedarwood's sweet, woody scent is known as a calming, grounding essential oil with reputed aphrodisiac effects. Use it when you're lacking confidence and want to set the world on fire.

*Clary sage (Salvia sclarea)*
Known for inducing euphoria, clary sage has the ability to balance while strengthening and relaxing. It is a reputed hormone balancer for women. If you're out of sorts or suffering from PMS, mix this into your witch's brew.

*Ginger (Zingiber officinale)*
Warming and stimulating, ginger is ideal for an activating and energizing massage. Known as an oil of initiation, it's traditionally associated with the planet Mars, which in astrology is symbolic of force and virility. Use this if you want action and you want it fast.

*continued*

*continued from previous page*

### Jasmine (Jasminum grandiflorum)

A sweet, euphoric scent with musky undertones, jasmine reawakens passion and releases inhibitions. The long-lasting, stimulating, and heart-opening oil is the sacred flower to the Hindu god of love, Kama.

### Neroli (Citrus aurantium)

A reputed aphrodisiac, this uplifting, calming essential oil is known for its powers of attraction for both men and woman. The orange blossoms were once used as an identifying scent for prostitutes in Madrid. Naughty!

### Orange (Citrus aurantium)

This luscious oil, expressed from the rind of the orange, is known for its uplifting and refreshing qualities, eliciting cheerful optimism and lightheartedness.

### Patchouli (Pogostemon cablin)

A beautiful oil that gets better with age. Grounding and enriching, this rich, woody scented oil is said to promote physical stamina and sexual potency. Some associate it with Grateful Dead shows, however.

### Rose absolute (Rosa centifolia)

Rose is renowned as the symbolic flower of love and sacred to Aphrodite, the Greek goddess of love of beauty. The soft gentle scent of rose opens the heart, encourages trust, and reinforces a sense of well-being.

### Rose geranium (Pelargonium graveolens)

A sharp, refreshing oil with green and rosy notes, rose geranium is known for encouraging intimacy and receptivity, for invoking love and happiness, and for strengthening balance and stability. It's a nice "getting to the next level" scent.

*Sandalwood (Santalum album)*
Want to smell like a walking advertisement for sex? Used in perfumes through the ages, sandalwood symbolizes unity and well-being. This essential oil, distilled from the heartwood and roots of the sandalwood tree, is often regarded as one of the most aphrodisiac of all botanicals.

*Tuberose absolute (Polianthes tuberosa)*
This is a dense, heavy floral scent with hypnotic, intriguing charm. Known for inducing sensuality and sensitivity, this wonderful aphrodisiac encourages expression while inspiring spontaneity. Use it when you're not sure how you want things to unfold and want to remain impetuous.

*Vanilla CO$_2$ (Vanilla planifolia)*
A versatile, sweet balsamic oil that warms and comforts, it is said to bring its subjects to sexual ecstasy of both body and mind. It's thought to be particularly attractive to men.

*Vetiver (Chrysopogon zizanioides)*
Vetiver oil is steam distilled from the roots of vetiver grass, symbolic for restoration and reconnection. This rich, woody, masculine oil, worn in India for thousands of years, is a known aphrodisiac, and is also used to promote tranquility and balance. If you're stuck in your head but want to be in your body, use this scent.

*Ylang-ylang complete (Cananga odorata)*
Steam distilled from the freshly picked flowers of *Cananga odorata*, this sweet, seductive flower complements all other flower oils it is combined with. Used to help its wearers slow down and appreciate the moment, ylang-ylang is deeply sensual and can create a sense of euphoria. If you want a taste of ecstasy, use a bit of this oil.

# DIY Massage Oil with Three Essential Scents

*What are the three scents one should never live without? Focus on sandalwood for its primal earthiness, rose with its heart-opening beauty, and vanilla to render your partner powerless. These three can also blend beautifully into a sensual massage oil.*

4 drops sandalwood essential oil
4 drops rose absolute essential oil
4 drops vanilla $CO_2$ essential oil
$1/4$ ounce ($1 1/2$ teaspoons) organic grape seed oil
$1/2$ ounce (1 tablespoon) organic almond oil

## For the Busy Bee Who Still Wants to Smell Like a Rose

Don't have time to make your own blends? There are some excellent, truly natural perfume brands on the market.

**Strange Invisible Perfumes** (siperfumes.com/sip): This completely botanical fragrance house, founded by Alexandra Balahoutis in Los Angeles, uses organic, wild-crafted, and biodynamic essences set in a base of 100 percent organic, beverage-grade grape alcohol. Her divine scents linger on the skin and are devastatingly sexy.

**Acorelle Natural Beauty** (lushoasis.com): The French know what they're doing, even when it comes to natural perfumes. This line of

Ecocert-certified perfumes uses organic wheat alcohol, floral water, plant extracts, and essential oils harvested from organic blossoms and fruits. There are seven scents, each one delightful in its own way.

**Red Flower** (redflower.com): This company's pure flower and herb distillations are handcrafted from USDA-certified organic oil. These are as close as you can get to high-end commercial scents, and the price tag matches the ambitions of the collection. Worth it if you can afford it!

Your skin is now glowing and you've passed the smell test with flying colors. Now that you're gussied up and gorgeous, it's time to slip into something more comfortable. Oh, wait—you're supposed to say that after you get your date back to your place. Regardless, the next chapter will take you through the ins and outs of eco-fashion.

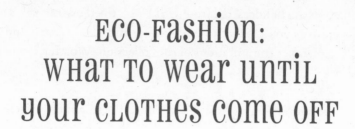

# chapter three

# ECO-Fashion:
# what to wear until
# your clothes come off

I f you hear one more person say that green is the new black, you're going to scream, aren't you? It's true, however, that finding eco-chic fashion is easier than ever. In fact, fashion-week events worldwide are now including eco-catwalks in addition to the traditional ones. And designers with real skills are using green fabrics. Even Pamela Anderson, animal rights activist and PETA supporter, has a new eco-clothing line, called A*Muse, in conjunction with former Heatherette designer Richie Rich.

Whether it's because of consumer demand or driven by marketing-related opportunism, you can now find well-made, cutting-edge, sexy clothes that won't kill the planet. From vintage to natural fibers, and from regenerated protein to recycled polyester, there are a ton of options for the eco-fashionista on the make—shoes and bags included.

# Vintage:
# What Comes Around Goes Around
# (and Still Looks Quite Sexy)

Of all your fashion options, buying vintage is the greenest. It covers all three of the Rs in the "reduce, reuse, recycle" triumvirate. You're reducing pollution when you don't buy into the production cycle, reusing something that's already made, and recycling it at the same time. Freaked out by used clothing? Just consider it preloved. If you're grossed out by the idea of wearing someone else's castaways (even if they've been thoroughly cleaned), you'll be glad to know that there is plenty of vintage clothing available that's never been worn. Called "dead stock," these are the items the manufacturer never sold, or that the store couldn't sell. You can find dead stock in most high-quality vintage stores. If you're shopping at Goodwill or the Salvation Army, you're most likely looking at items that have spent some time on others' bodies or in their closets. Shopping vintage offers a fun way to try on personalities from a different era or culture—you can be a totally new you any night of the week without having to shell out thousands of dollars on designer duds. And a trade secret of fashion houses is that the top designers often look to vintage clothing for inspiration for each new season's designs.

## Make It New

If you're a pack rat, you may be in luck—you can go vintage shopping in your own closet. Even if something from one or two seasons ago feels dated now, you can dress it up with accessories, cut it up, belt it, sew on new buttons, or dye it with a natural dye. Or just hold on to it for another few years—there's a good chance it will come back into style eventually. If you feel the need to buy new, go with simple, classic styles in the interest of longevity. The LBD (little black dress) never goes out of fashion.

# What's New Is New Again: Eco-Chic Fashion

The first thing to know about products labeled "green" or "eco-friendly" is that many of them aren't. Eco-fashionistas must do their homework. So let's look at the fabrics that genuine green designers are using these days.

## Fabric: A Short Course in Green Textiles

Learning which sustainably produced textiles are most accessible and comfortable is a good place to start when trying to green your wardrobe. Some are natural and some are synthetic, but they're all probably better than most of what's in the local department store.

### Natural Fibers

**Bamboo:** This wonderfully soft, silky, antimicrobial fabric is a dream for fashion designers because of its lovely draping qualities. It's also wrinkle resistant and takes dyes more easily than other fabrics. But debates are raging about how eco-friendly bamboo really is. In one camp are the people who believe that, as a rapidly renewable resource, bamboo wins points for oxygenating the atmosphere and reducing greenhouse gases; plus, it doesn't require pesticides or fertilizers to grow. In the other camp are people who say that the problem is not with bamboo growing but with bamboo processing, which often employs harsh chemicals that leach into soil and water. Most bamboo is processed in China, where the industry is still fairly unregulated. There is no Forest Stewardship Council for bamboo, so it's iffy whether bamboo, almost exclusively from China, is sustainable. One way to get around this problem is to look for bamboo linen, which is mechanically processed and doesn't rely on chemicals. Demand bamboo fabric that isn't coated with any softener, such as silicone, and does not have Lycra or spandex added.

**Hemp:** It's not just for smoking. By the far the greenest fabric, hemp grows without pesticides, herbicides, or fertilizers and has low water requirements. It also matures in one season, has deep roots that assist in controlling soil erosion, and produces 250 percent more fibers per acre than cotton. Hemp has the feel of cotton but is more durable and absorbent.

**Organic cotton:** It's better than pesticide-laden conventional cotton, but it still has very high water requirements. Look for cotton from regions of the world where the plant is indigenous, so that rain covers most of the water needs: Mexico, Peru, India, China, portions of Africa—basically, the tropics and subtropics. Don't buy cotton produced in an area that is not at least subtropical.

**Organic wool:** The organic wool trade association says that, in order to qualify for their seal, producers must use organic livestock feed for their little lambs and allow them to forage; avoid use of synthetic hormones, genetic engineering, and synthetic pesticides (internal, external, and on pastures); and encourage livestock health through good cultural and management practices.

**Organic flax linen:** If you go with flax linen, be careful that it's not made from synthetic fiber, which is common these days. Flax doesn't require a lot of irrigation, which saves water for those sensuous baths you'll want to take once the organic flax linen comes off.

## Regenerated Protein Fibers

**Soy and soy silk:** This protein fiber absorbs dye well, so vegetable dyes can effectively be used. Chemicals are used to process the fabric, similar to the way bamboo is processed, but the chemicals are less harsh. Soy and soy silk employ a *closed-loop* system of manufacturing, which means that all of the components that go into and all by-products from making the fabrics are completely compostable. But soy is often grown with pesticides and may be a *genetically modified organism* (GMO) unless it's organic. On the other hand, the fabric uses a waste product (soy bean hulls), something that would otherwise be thrown out.

**Cork:** Are you a leather lover? If you like the look and feel of biker chic but don't want any animals to die for your style, look into cork. Cork is the spongy inner bark of an oak tree native to the Mediterranean. It can be harvested every nine to twelve years without harm to the tree that produces it. It was a popular fabric in the mid-1800s and is now

CLOSED LOOP: According to the Dictionary of Sustainable Management, a closed-loop supply chain is a zero-waste system. All materials must be completely reused, recycled, or composted. (The term is sometimes used to describe companies that are responsible for the waste they produce.)[17]

GENETICALLY MODIFIED ORGANISM: Commonly known as a GMO, this is an organism whose genetic material has been altered using genetic engineering. Also referred to as "franken foods," GMO crops are considered dangerous by many.

making a comeback amongst eco-designers. (Just make sure it's not treated with Scotchgard, a common practice with this material.)

**Ingeo:** This is a polylactic acid made into fabric. Patagonia decided against using the corn-based fabric because Ingeo relies, at least partially, on GMO corn. It is not biodegradable, but it is compostable under specified humidity and temperature conditions. Currently it's difficult to find non-GMO versions of this fabric, but we can hope that this will change over time.

## Regenerated Cellulose Fibers

These fabrics are basically rayon, but they use a closed-loop manufacturing process, and they require fewer toxic chemicals than conventional rayon does.

**Lyocell and tencel:** Made from wood pulp, this fabric's production process is very eco-friendly (a closed-loop use of chemicals that aren't all that toxic). However, it doesn't take dyes well, so the coloring stage can involve lots of chemicals. It is soft, strong, and resistant to wrinkles, and it feels and drapes a bit like rayon, so a lot of eco-designers enjoy working with it.

**Modal:** Modal is made from the pulp of beech wood, with production techniques similar to those used for Lyocell.

## Recycled Synthetic Fiber

Polyethylene terephthalate, also called EcoSpun, Eco-fi, or Capilene (made from recycled plastic bottles), is endorsed by the Sierra Club. This fabric isn't biodegradable like those made with vegetable and protein fibers, but we need to do something with all the excess bottles. The fleece made from this substance is very soft and warm.

# Certifiable: Green Textile Credentials

Textile certification is still a messy affair. The certification landscape is strewn with a mishmash of organizations, each with its own unique method of measuring the eco-friendliness of various brands. The certification bodies listed below are often found on clothing labels, and all should be considered good signs of the garment's greenness, but none of them can be considered the gold standard quite yet. For more information, see also the list of certifying agencies in chapter 1.

- ✦ Bluesign
- ✦ Control Union Certifiers (formerly SKAL)
- ✦ Ecological and Toxicological Association of Dyes and Organic Pigments Manufacturers (ETAD)
- ✦ Oeko-Tex Standard 100

## Etsy and eBay Put the Two E's in Green

You know about eBay, of course. Perhaps you've used it for electronics or tchotchke shopping. It's heaven on earth for snagging hard-to-find vintage pieces if your local shops aren't cutting it. (Just make sure your seller favors environmentally friendly shipping.)

Now meet the new(ish) girl on the block, Etsy. Etsy.com is site dedicated to building a new economy based on handmade goods. Tons of greenies buy and sell their wares here, and many eco-designers prefer it. So check it out, and don't expect to leave empty-handed. Cute overload!

# Eco-Friendly Designers of Note

Below is a list of the lovely folks who follow Tim Gunn's counsel to "make it work" flawlessly. The designers in this section are real pioneers, because their industry is still a very traditional one. Clothing manufacture is largely still a mass-production affair taking place mostly in China and Bangladesh in less-than-ideal working conditions. However, it can be done the way these trailblazers do it: clean and green.

## Eco-Lingerie: Know What's in Your Knickers

Anything that makes contact with your nether regions should be made of nothing but the good stuff. Because bamboo is antibacterial and prevents odors, it's an excellent choice in panties.

**Urban Fox** (urbanfoxeco.com) knows undies. This Midwestern line creates supercute, always sexy, and slightly edgy lingerie from machine-pressed bamboo and organic cotton blends. They are designed, dyed, and sewn by hand in the good old USA. The company's garters and thigh-high tights take you back to another era, and you won't want to leave.

**Cosabella** (cosabella.com), a trusted name in all things sexy, now makes an eco-friendly line with low-impact bamboo and natural vegetable color dyes. The panties, chemises, camis, and pajama sets are soft and delectable.

**Eco-Boudoir** (eco-boudoir.com) is a UK-based company making bamboo, organic cotton, and silk lingerie certified by Control Union

Certifiers. Production is based in Britain, but the company sometimes employs small cooperatives of women abroad.

**Peau-ethique** (peau-ethique.com) sells adorable organic cotton fair-trade underthings for the boudoir with that irresistible French flair.

## Shoes

These are not your mother's Birkenstocks. "Earth-friendly shoes" no longer means heinous, clunky sandals worn with socks. Today, designers are rocking some seriously stylish shoes that won't harm Mama Earth.

**Mohop** sandals (mohops.com) are made by Annie Mohaupt, a woman on an eco-fashion mission. Her amazing sandals are adorable, sexy, and infinitely recyclable. Her shoes have been dubbed the "infinity sandal," because the wearer can easily customize her shoes by changing the ribbons used for tying them. Different lengths and styles of ribbons can be used to achieve a virtually infinite number of looks with just one pair of wooden soles. Depending on your mood, you can go good-girl pretty with daintily tied pink or red ribbons, or bad-girl vixen with S&M-style black ribbons tied high on the ankle.

**Olsen Haus Pure Vegan** (olsenhaus.com) uses plant-based and human-made nonanimal materials that are alternative, sustainable, and renewable. This line is 100 percent vegan: no leather, fur, wool, or silk is ever used. And the shoes will rock your world. Totally edgy, incredibly chic, and ultrasexy. The soles are a composite of rubber, the glues are rubber based and vegan, and the paint is vegan and nontoxic. (Why vegan? As we'll discuss in chapter 4, every person eating a vegan diet saves at least an acre of trees every year.)

**Mink** (minkshoes.com), the ironically named vegan shoe line created by Rebecca Mink, is all kinds of fabulous. This line is handmade in Italy by an artisan shoe cobbler, employing materials like cork, denim, linen, and faux fur. They're not cheap, but you can consider them your eco-friendly Manolos.

## Fabrics Direct!

DIY much? Here's a list of Organic Trade Association members who sell organic fabric directly to consumers either by mail order or online:

Anna Sova Luxury Organics: annasova.com

Chandler & Greene: chandlergreene.com

Cotton Plus: organiccottonplus.com

Dream Designs: dreamdesigns.ca

Earth Friendly Goods: earthfriendlygoods.com

Furnature: furnature.com

Greenfibre: greenfibres.com

Green Mountain Spinnery: spinnery.com

Harmony Art: harmonyart.com

Mod Green Pod: modgreenpod.com

NearSea Naturals: nearseanaturals.com

# Bags

If you're only willing to do vintage in one area of your closet, make it your handbags. Mothers and grandmothers and aunts tend to be very helpful here. If you don't have access to vintage bag booty, scout them at the local Salvation Army or vintage consignment stores. You'd better believe that old ladies who were the fashionistas of their day are getting rid of their stuff all the time. Don't let it go to the landfill.

Must buy new? Check out these awesome eco-chic purse purveyors.

**Ecoist** (ecoist.com) handbags are made from recycled candy wrappers, food packages, soda labels, subway maps, newspapers, and other landfill-bound materials. Their chic clutches make eye-catching evening bags.

**Matt & Nat** (mattandnat.com) makes beautifully designed handbags that are totally vegan and totally on trend. All the linings of the bags are made from recycled soda bottles. This company makes sexy clutches, top handles, wallets, shoulder bags, and overnighters for that weekend away with your lover.

**Remade USA** (remadeusa.com) takes old leather and makes it into your new, chic, one-of-a-kind purse. You can even send them your own castaway—they'll remake it for you and give you a discount.

# Clothes

Although department stores and chains are getting on the eco-bandwagon, most still use mass-manufacturing overseas. So, just as you try to eat locally, try your best to shop for clothes made and sold locally. More and more small shops are following the trend toward in-house, local manufacturing. Seek out stores like Kaight Shop (kaightshop.com) in New York City, which proudly boasts the "Made in Brooklyn" label on many of its styles. Try to find classic styles and clothes that are well made and will last for many seasons.

**ecoSkin** (ecoskincollections.com) is a Los Angeles–based line of supersexy and body-skimming dresses—the ideal date clothes. They're made of eco-friendly materials like bamboo, hemp, and organic cotton.

**The Four Hundred** (showroomfourhundred.com) is the only eco-friendly designer showroom in New York City. All the lines shown there are absolutely gorgeous, ultrachic, and as conscious as you can get. Bahar Shahpar's sustainable collection is just one of the green

## Keeping Green Clothes Clean: Percs Have No Perks

When it comes to cleaning your new (or old) eco-duds, beware the traditional dry cleaner. That smell on your freshly dry-cleaned clothing comes from tetrachloroethylene, a central nervous system depressant that's been known to leach into soil and groundwater around dry-cleaning facilities. It's known to cause dizziness, headache, sleepiness, confusion, nausea, difficulty speaking and walking, unconsciousness, and death. If you're buying new or vintage, try to find fabrics that don't require dry-cleaning. Ask your local cleaners what their method is, and find out if there are any shops that use $CO_2$ cleaning—it's a much greener alternative to dry-cleaning your clothes. In the meantime, if you've got lots of cashmere in your closet, spot clean when you can. If you simply must use your traditional dry cleaner once in a while, at least ask the clerks not to wrap your garment in plastic or paper for pickup.

brands on display. Her clothing is produced locally in New York, one of the emerging green fashion capitals of the world. The styles are sexy, playful, and feminine.

**Loyale Clothing** (loyaleclothing.com) by Jenny Hwa is a terrific line of sustainable casual wear that is great for daytime dates. She uses organic cotton, factory-reclaimed overstock fabrics, and color-grown organic cotton.

If you're not sure where to start your green shopping expedition, try searching on ecofashionworld.com. This website has an excellent "Browse by Eco Criteria" function that lists lines that fall into these categories: vegetarian and animal free, ethically produced, craft and artisan, custom or tailor-made, fair-trade certified, organic, recycled, and vintage and secondhand. You can find designers that meet both your fashion and green needs here. In addition, get yourself on Rachel Sarnoff's amazing EcoStilleto.com mailing list, so you are always on top of the latest trends.

Now you're glossed, perfumed, and dressed to the nines in head-to-toe green wear. Isn't it time for sex yet? Nope, you and your lovebird have got to eat first. The next chapter will show you how to serve it up eco-friendly.

# CHAPTER FOUR

# ECO-LICIOUS APHRODISIAC FOODS: THE CREAM OF THE CROP

*Eat food. Not too much. Mostly plants.*
—Michael Pollan

Our fast-food-addicted culture says a lot about who we are—not just about the state of our health and our attention spans, but also about the sorry state of our sex lives. "Wham, bam, thank you, ma'am" is our mantra, while sitting on our ever-expanding fannies in the drive-through line at McDonalds and in our drive-through bedrooms (where three to thirteen minutes of intercourse is the standard). This isn't surprising. At the end of a long day during which you've consumed little real nutrition, who has energy for foreplay? It's just one more ugly symptom of our collective malaise. Americans are overwhelmingly obese, suffer from diabetes, have heart conditions, and are decidedly unsexy—because we eat food that is not really food. The processed foods available in our supermarkets are irradiated, made with GMOs and high-fructose corn syrup, and feature "fat-free" options with just barely edible chemical mixtures.

Michael Pollan calls the food industry's attempt to fake us out with Frankenfoods "nutritionism." On the other side of this unsavory situation are a growing number of hypervigilant consumers who want to be healthy, slim, and sexy. But many of them take it too far. A spirit of denial drills the sensuality out of eating. Why not enjoy equal parts pleasure and good health?

Eco-sexuals need to know what *not* to eat, but they should also know what *to* eat, and how to eat it with gusto. The slow food movement is an excellent place to start. Most of us live to work instead of working to live. But the slow food movement aims to change all that, and it's getting there, bite by bite.

# The Slow Food Movement and Eco-Sex: A Match Made in a Very Sexy Version of Heaven

Incorporating a slow foods approach into your life seems to make time magically expand. It may take more time to source your vegetables and cook your lover's dinner, but it's entirely worth it. Those who adhere to cooking and eating the slow way believe that this practice enhances all five senses—touch, taste, smell, sound, and sight—which can lead to erotic, sustained lovemaking.

The slow food movement has been around since 1989, and true to its name, it lazily wound its way into the gastronomic hearts of top chefs worldwide over the course of about twenty years. With more than 100,000 members in 132 countries, the organization is a wealth of juicy information for would-be eco-sexuals who want to green their pantries, not just their panties. The slow food mission is to remind people of where their food actually comes from. Most of us don't stop to think about this as we rush through the supermarket throwing stuff into our carts. Slow-foodists encourage us to shop at the local farmers' market or, if your town lacks one, to find local growers who are willing to deliver. Even if your only option is a big-box supermarket, flex your consumer muscle and ask for local food. You can also join a local CSA (community supported agriculture) cooperative. Find the one closest to you at localharvest.org/csa.

Slow-foodists believe in biodiversity and something they call "taste education." Most of us have totally lost touch with our senses because of overconsumption of highly processed foods, so we need to go back to the basics. (In chapter 8 we'll look what it really means to eat sensually.)

## Keep It Local

*Locavore*, the 2007 word of the year in the *Oxford American Dictionary*, is usually defined as someone who believes that food must be grown within a one-hundred-mile radius of the place it is consumed. A *locavore* is naturally a slow-foodist. An incredibly sexy outgrowth of locavore culture is the supper club, where people get together to sample dinners made of local foods, sometimes by up-and-coming chefs, at locations typically undisclosed until the night of the event.

You can take the locavore movement one step farther and grow your own. The strawberry picked from your balcony or your backyard is even fresher than the one picked yesterday by your favorite local farmer. Picking fruit together—what's sexier? You may think that you're simply not a candidate for microfarming, but even the smallest bits of outdoor space can accommodate gardens (even fire-escape gardens can thrive in the brutal environs of New York City, if they are cared for well). *Fresh Food from Small Spaces*, by R. J. Ruppenthal, is but one book that can show you how to up your local foods ante. And if you do live in a cold climate and can't grow year-round, you can learn how to can your foods. Check out *Well-Preserved* by Eugenia Bone for tips.

# Organic Foods

A funny thing about the organic "movement" is that it's actually the way we have eaten through most of our agricultural history. It was only in the twentieth century that chemicals were introduced and came to rule our farms. Early proponents of organic food went by the mantra "Know your farmer, know your food," but now you can pick up a bag of organic carrots at Walmart.

Organic food is still more expensive, and even controversial. Michelle Obama's organic garden was targeted by lobbyists from the

## Grow Your Own

Here's a ridiculously easy tip for starting your own garden. All you need are organic seeds or transplants and a bag of topsoil. Cut off the top of the bag and make some drainage holes in the bottom and sides with some scissors. Plant your seeds or plants, and voilà—your own personal low-maintenance garden.

pesticide industry when she first broke ground in early 2009. The row between conventional (nonorganic) farmers and organic farmers will exist as long as both are options. (The hope is that eventually all food will be produced organically.) Whether or not organic food is indeed more nutritious, as many believe, it has been established that pesticides are not just dangerous, but horrible for the planet. Chemical runoff into waterways is but one frightening catastrophe caused by conventional farming every season, not to mention the oil that pesticides are made with. And, of course, pesticides, herbicides, and insecticides don't just live on the skin of your strawberry. Some of the substances can be washed off, but still more seeps into the fruit's flesh and then into your flesh after you've consumed it. Simply put, they're bad news. If you can afford it, buy organic. If we ask for it, one day it will be more affordable—it's the old supply-and-demand saw.

# Going Raw

Living and raw foods are green because they use little or no heat in their preparation. And almost nothing is processed—a raw foods diet is mainly based on fruits, seeds, veggies, and nuts. And damn, is it delicious. Its premise is that foods' natural vital enzymes are cooked out of existence when food is heated over 116 degrees Fahrenheit. Because enzymes help us digest and absorb nutrients, much of the cooked food that we eat does nothing but rot in our stomach, according to raw-foodists. Many people who go raw never go back. Raw-foodists tend to have a gorgeous glow, and with it comes a fervor for their diet and lifestyle. If you're a sensually oriented foodie who scoffs at anyone who would choose to survive on veggies, fruits, and nuts, your mind will be blown when you see the recipes from Sarma Melngailis, of Pure Food and Wine, later in the chapter.

# Vegetarianism and Beyond

Warning: The next few paragraphs are decidedly unsexy, but necessary.

Why give up meat? Look into the eyes of Fido or Fluffy and you'll see why. Or, if that doesn't move you, think about the enormous amount of resources used for meat production. Did you know that most of the grain produced in the United States is fed to cattle? One brief glance into the ugly underbelly of agribusiness is enough to cause many to give up meat, or at least to give up factory-farmed meat. According to Farm Sanctuary (farmsanctuary.org):

> The quantity of waste produced by farm animals in the U.S. is more than 130 times greater than that produced by humans. Agricultural runoff has killed millions of fish, and is the main reason why 60 percent of America's rivers and streams are "impaired." In states with concentrated animal agriculture, the waterways have become rife with pfiesteria bacteria. In addition to killing fish, pfiesteria causes open sores, nausea, memory loss, fatigue and disorientation in humans. Even groundwater, which takes thousands of years to restore, is being contaminated. For example, the aquifer under the San Bernardino Dairy Preserve in southern California contains more nitrates and other pollutants than water coming from sewage treatment plants.[18]

It's not just about pollution, however. Livestock production accounts for 8 percent of global human water use.[19] Since many people believe that the next big war will be fought over water, this is a key issue for all of us, both ethically and environmentally. Clearly, eating conventional meat is bad for the environment. But ethics also offer plenty of sexy reasons to go vegetarian, too. The evils of agribusiness are a great persuader for anyone still on the fence about giving up meat. In the United States alone, nine million chickens, pigs, turkeys, calves, and cows are slaughtered every day. If supermarkets showed videos of what goes on at most factory farms, they'd probably have few takers for those packaged chicken parts on Styrofoam trays. The beef industry is notoriously abusive (but they have a powerful lobby in congress—just ask Oprah, who was sued by Texas cattle ranchers for saying that she'd never eat another hamburger on her show back in 1996). Beef cattle are still branded, for tracking purposes, the way that they were by early pioneers. When their skin is burned, they cry out—a not-so-fun fact to think about the next time you're tempted to chow down on a burger. Some cows are left to die in freezing cold and inclement weather on the range, while others are herded up and sold at auction for slaughter. This is all in addition to the horrible conditions that animals raised for meat are forced to endure, including overcrowding, beak cutting, tail cutting (cows), and being made to sit in a stew of toxins and decaying manure. This is a list of the milder infractions, by the way—it gets far worse, but this is a book about sex, so I don't want to turn you off for the rest of the year.

## Going Vegan: Because Loving Animals Is Sexy

Veganism isn't just a diet; it's a lifestyle choice. Vegans use only animal-free products across the board; they will not wear or sleep on anything made with wool or silk, nor will they eat anything with casein, a dairy derivative. A dedicated vegan once told me why he would never drink cow's milk. He explained that even if he personally met the cow and knew that it was treated with love and respect, grazed on grass, and had a fabulous life, he still couldn't bring himself to drink its milk. Why? When we're sipping a latte, we don't often think about the fact that cows have to be artificially inseminated in order to keep lactating. (In fact, a common dairy industry term for the restraints used during this process is the "rape rack.") Vegans are not people to be trifled with; they are committed, serious animal lovers. If you're searching for someone who knows the true meaning of selflessness in bed, look no further than a vegan. All that passion is incredibly sexy.

If you're all about having a buff bod, just listen to the authors of *Skinny Bitch*—a purely vegan diet is one of the fastest ways to lose weight.

## Some Sexy Vegans and Vegetarians of Note

| | | |
|---|---|---|
| Alicia Silverstone | Emily Deschanel | Natalie Portman |
| Alyssa Milano | Gillian Anderson | Pamela Anderson |
| André 3000 | Ginnifer Goodwin | Portia de Rossi |
| Brandy | Jennifer Connelly | Prince |
| Carrie Anne Moss | Joaquin Phoenix | Sandra Oh |
| Casey Affleck | Kristen Bell | Tea Leoni |
| Demi Moore | Milo Ventimiglia | Vanessa A. Williams |
| Elijah Wood | Moby | Woody Harrelson |

# Fruit of the Sea

The humble pescatarian has issues these days. Although seafood is widely thought to have myriad health benefits (witness the fish oil craze), it has been harvested unsustainably for so long that many fisheries are threatened with collapse worldwide. And the mercury found in many of the most delicious and readily available fish can be harmful for pregnant women and anyone with a compromised immune system. The Monterey Bay Aquarium is on the job, however. Their handy and regularly updated Seafood Watch Pocket Guide (montereybayaquarium.org/cr/cr_seafoodwatch/download.aspx) is downloadable from their website, is broken down by region, and also includes sushi recommendations. (It's also available as an iPhone app.)

# Serving Up Seduction

There are so many aphrodisiac foods, and it would be a shame not to stir them up for a dinner date! When experimenting with all the recipes in this section, always aim to use organic, locally grown foods when possible. Each of these recipes has at least one gender-specific aphrodisiac ingredient (see the lists on the following page). They're also designed to be highly sensual and erotic in their presentation, texture, and taste.

## How to Seduce a Man with an Eco-Friendly Meal

Sarma Melngailis, proprietor and cofounder of New York's Pure Food and Wine restaurant, is one sexy chef. She's the author of *Raw Food/Real World* (Harper Collins, 2005) and *Living Raw Food: Get the Glow with More Recipes from Pure Food and Wine* (Harper Collins, 2009). Sarma also runs the online eco-haven One Lucky Duck (oneluckyduck.com). Here are a few of her come-hither recipes.

Aphrodisiacs, named for Aphrodite, goddess of love, are thought not just to pump up the libido but also to make sex more pleasurable. But forget Spanish fly (made from mashed, dried beetles) and stick with tried-and-true foods and herbs that are delicious, organic, and easily obtainable at the health food store.

## Aphrodisiac Foods for Women

| | | | |
|---|---|---|---|
| Almond | Basil | Ginger | Soy |
| Angelica | Cardamom | Licorice | Truffles |
| Artichokes | Chocolate | Papaya | |
| Avocado | Damiana | Saffron | |

## Aphrodisiac Foods for Men

| | | | |
|---|---|---|---|
| Basil | Cnidium seeds | Grapes | Pineapple |
| Bay leaf | Fennel | Hemp seeds | Pumpkin |
| Cardamom | Figs | Lavender | Sea cucumber |
| Cayenne | Ginger | Mango | Squash |
| Celery | Ginkgo | Mustard | Vanilla |
| Chiles | Ginseng | Nutmeg | Watermelon |
| Cinnamon | Goji berries | Peach | |

# Vanilla Salad Starter

*This recipe, created by Sarma exclusively for eco-sexuals, is a blend of baby arugula, mâche, and shaved fennel topped with a sensuous vanilla-bean vinaigrette and cinnamon figs, pistachios, mint, and parsley. If baby arugula or mâche is unavailable, try butter lettuce or any other local tender and mild baby greens as a good substitute.*

*The recipe yields more vinaigrette than you need here—save the remainder to use on other light greens or salad. Banyuls vinegar from France is golden in color with a distinct flavor that is mellower than other red wine vinegars. Use another high-quality red or white wine vinegar if Banyuls is unavailable.*

## VANILLA BEAN VINAIGRETTE

$^1/_2$ cup Banyuls vinegar

$1^1/_2$ teaspoons agave nectar

2 teaspoons sea salt

Seeds scraped from $^3/_4$ vanilla bean

1 cup extra-virgin olive oil

$^1/_3$ cup almond oil or other high-quality nut oil

4 ripe black mission figs

1 tablespoon agave nectar

Pinch of cinnamon

Fine sea salt

$^1/_4$ cup coarsely chopped pistachios

1 teaspoon nut oil

2 cups baby arugula

2 cups mâche

1 tablespoon coarsely chopped fresh mint

1 very small handful fresh parsley leaves

To make the vinaigrette, put the vinegar, agave nectar, salt, and vanilla seeds in a blender and process until completely smooth. In a small bowl, combine the olive oil and almond oil. With the blender running, slowly pour the oils into the dressing and continue to blend until emulsified.

Next, cut the figs into quarters and place in a small bowl. Add the agave nectar, cinnamon, and a pinch of salt, and toss very gently.

Toss the pistachios in another small bowl with the nut oil and a pinch of salt.

Place the greens, mint, parsley, and pistachios with their oil into a mixing bowl and add enough of the vinaigrette to coat the leaves. Toss very gently. Taste and adjust the seasoning if needed. To serve, divide the greens and pistachios between two plates and top with the figs.

Yield: 2 servings

## Chanterelle and Yuzu Ceviche

*Ceviche is a traditional Peruvian dish that uses the acids in fruits (most commonly limes and lemons) to denature the proteins of raw fish or seafood. Although the dish is raw, the chemical action of the acid partially cooks the fish without the use of heat. The same technique can be applied to most mushrooms, in this case, wild chanterelles. We add the juice from the Japanese citrus fruit yuzu to the marinade for an exotic flavor. The juice is available at most Asian markets: if you can't find it, simply use more of the other citrus juices.*

*Layered with the creamy, sweet pineapple-avocado puree and moderately spicy salsa, this is a cool and light starter (with just the right amount of zest for you and your date). The multicolored heirloom tomatoes, available in the summer, make the dish even prettier.*

## CHANTERELLE CEVICHE

3 tablespoons freshly squeezed orange juice

3 tablespoons freshly squeezed lemon juice

3 tablespoons freshly squeezed lime juice

1 tablespoon yuzu juice

$1^1/_2$ teaspoons sea salt

2 tablespoons extra-virgin olive oil

2 or 3 scallions, green parts only, thinly sliced

Freshly ground black pepper

4 cups whole chanterelle mushrooms

## PINEAPPLE-AVOCADO PUREE

$1^1/_2$ cups chopped fresh pineapple (about $^1/_2$ small pineapple)

$1^1/_2$ ripe, yet firm, avocados, peeled and pitted

$^3/_4$ teaspoon sea salt

## HEIRLOOM CHERRY TOMATO SALSA

3 cups heirloom cherry tomatoes, sliced into halves

$^3/_4$ cup finely diced celery (save the celery hearts for garnish)

$^1/_2$ small bunch parsley (about 1 cup), leaves only, roughly chopped, plus additional sprigs for garnish

1 jalapeño, seeded and finely minced

2 scallions, white part and 1 inch of green, sliced very thin

$1^1/_2$ teaspoons red wine vinegar

$1^1/_2$ teaspoons extra-virgin olive oil

$^1/_2$ teaspoon sea salt

To make the ceviche marinade, place the orange, lemon, and lime juices, yuzu juice, and salt in a blender and blend until well mixed. (It's important to blend the salt with the juices very well so the mushrooms will properly break down while marinating. If you don't feel like using a blender, whisk the mixture thoroughly and make sure the salt is fully dissolved.)

Transfer the mixture to a bowl and whisk in the olive oil, scallions, and pepper to taste.

To prepare the chanterelle mushrooms, first cut off the coarse end of the stem. Then cut the mushrooms into halves or quarters, depending upon the size. Place the cut mushrooms into a bowl of cold water and massage with your hands to remove any dirt. Remove the mushrooms from the water and lay them out on paper towels. Pat the mushrooms dry.

Pour the marinade over the mushrooms and let them sit at least 30 minutes. Set aside.

Next, puree the pineapple in a blender until it becomes a smooth liquid. Add the avocados and sea salt and continue blending until very smooth. Set aside.

To make the salsa, place all the ingredients in a bowl and toss until evenly mixed.

To serve, set up 2 martini glasses. Place 2 to 3 tablespoons of pineapple-avocado puree in the bottom of each glass. Top with 3 to 4 tablespoons salsa, then about $1/4$ cup marinated mushrooms. Repeat once or twice, as needed. You'll have plenty extra for second helpings, if needed. Garnish with the parsley sprigs and celery heart stalks.

Yield: 4 cups

*Reprinted from* Living Raw Food, *by Sarma Melngailis, by permission of Harper-Collins Publishers. Copyright 2009 by 77 Lucky Cows, Inc.*

# Yellow Squash "Fettuccine" with Creamy Pine Nut Alfredo

*In the summer you can usually find goldbar squash, which is a lovely dark yellow variety that tastes great with the lemon basil and green olives. It's also shaped more like straight zucchini and so is easier to julienne. If goldbar is unavailable, regular yellow summer squash is fine. A small plastic mandoline slicer is a handy tool to have, and they're very inexpensive. If you don't have one, you can peel the squash with a vegetable peeler into thin strips, but this will take a while.*

**CREAMY PINE NUT ALFREDO SAUCE**
$1^1/_2$ cups raw pine nuts
3 tablespoons extra-virgin olive oil
$^1/_4$ cup freshly squeezed lemon juice
1 tablespoon nutritional yeast
$^1/_2$ teaspoon sea salt

2 or 3 medium goldbar or yellow summer squash
Sea salt
$^1/_4$ cup raw pine nuts
$^1/_2$ teaspoon nut oil or extra-virgin olive oil
$^1/_4$ cup green olives, pitted and thinly sliced
1 small handful of lemon basil leaves
Freshly ground black pepper

To make the Alfredo sauce, place the pine nuts in a bowl and add enough water to cover. Let sit for 1 hour or more to plump the nuts.

Drain the pine nuts and put them in a blender with the olive oil, lemon juice, nutritional yeast, and salt. Blend until smooth. If the sauce is too thick, add a drizzle of water to thin it.

To make the "fettuccine," cut the ends off the squash. Julienne the squash on a mandoline and place it in a colander or strainer. Toss with about ½ teaspoon of sea salt and let sit for at least 30 minutes to soften and allow a bit of the liquid to drain out.

Chop the pine nuts and put them in a small bowl with the oil and a pinch of salt.

Place enough squash for two servings in a medium bowl. Add enough of the sauce to generously coat the "fettuccine". Add the green olives, half of the lemon basil, and a pinch of black pepper and gently toss.

Divide the "fettuccine" between two shallow bowls, making tall piles. Drizzle more of the sauce around the squash. Sprinkle with the chopped pine nuts and garnish with remaining basil leaves.

Yield: 2 cups

## Sarma Says, Get Him Drunk

*This cocktail, called the Master Cleanse–Tini in* Living Raw Food, *uses the flavor combination of healer Stanley Burroughs's Master Cleanse, or Lemonade Diet. This sake-tini is lemony-tart yet with a woodsy sweetness and a spicy kick. Take a sip and you'll be immediately invigorated!*

1½ cups sake
1½ cups freshly squeezed lemon juice
¾ cup filtered water
⅔ cup maple syrup
¼ teaspoon cayenne pepper
¼ cup coarse crystal date sugar

Combine all of the ingredients except the date sugar in a bowl or other container and mix to thoroughly combine.

Place the date sugar in a shallow bowl or small plate. Wet the rims of the martini glasses and dip them into the date sugar, as you would if you were salting the rims of glasses for a traditional margarita.

Shake the liquid over ice in a martini shaker and pour into the martini glasses.

Yield: 4 'tinis

*Reprinted from* Living Raw Food, *by Sarma Melngailis, by permission of Harper-Collins Publishers. Copyright 2009 by 77 Lucky Cows, Inc.*

CRGCRGCRGCRGCRGCRGCRGCRGCRGCRGCRGCRGCRGCRGCRGCRG

## Morning-After Breakfast: Cacao Nib Shake

*You got lucky. Here's what Sarma says you should serve him in bed. The sweetness of this shake will depend on the ripeness of the bananas you're using. The perfect banana is dark yellow, just before it starts to get the little brown spots. Ideally, you will peel the bananas the night before, cut or break into pieces, put them in a zippered bag or other container, and place in the freezer.*

2 heaping tablespoons raw cashew butter
2 cups cold filtered water
2 tablespoons agave nectar, plus more to taste
1 teaspoon vanilla extract
1 heaping teaspoon coconut butter or oil (optional)
Pinch of cinnamon
Pinch of salt
2 heaping tablespoons cocoa powder (preferably raw)
1 large or 2 small ripe bananas, cut into pieces and frozen
1 heaping tablespoon raw cacao nibs

Place the cashew butter, water, agave nectar, vanilla, coconut butter, cinnamon, and salt into a blender and process until smooth.

Add the cocoa powder and frozen banana and blend until smooth. Add the raw cacao nibs and blend until smooth. Raw cacao nibs will give the shake a little bit of crunchiness and an added caffeine kick.

Taste for sweetness and add more agave nectar if you like.

Yield: 2 generous shakes

## How to Seduce a Woman with an Eco-Friendly Meal

Bryant Terry uses the sensual pleasures of the table to inspire people to contribute to building a healthier, just, and sustainable food system. He is the author of *Vegan Soul Kitchen: Fresh, Healthy, and Creative African American Cuisine* and *Grub: Ideas for an Urban Organic Kitchen.* The following sensual South Asian supper, which he created just for us at Eco-Sex HQ, is infused with a number of herbs, spices, and vegetables to stimulate desire in your dinner date. Curry, the quintessential Indian dish, provides a perfect vehicle for "sneaking" in asparagus, sweet potatoes, garlic, and ginger—all purported aphrodisiacs. The turmeric-coated yellow rice is ideal for sopping up curry sauce, and the luscious lassi provides sweet creamy interludes in between peppery bites.

# Cardamom-Saffron Sweet Lassi

*This version of lassi—a traditional North Indian beverage made by blending yogurt with water, spices, and sometimes fruit—is mainly colored and flavored by saffron, a spice derived from the flower of the saffron crocus (Crocus sativus). Cardamom, the aromatic seeds of a plant in the ginger family, adds additional stimulation.*

4 whole cardamom pods
$1/8$ teaspoon saffron threads, crumbled,
   plus 2 pinches for garnish
$1/2$ cup boiling water
$1^1/2$ cups plain yogurt
$1/4$ cup coconut milk
3 to 4 tablespoons agave nectar
4 medium ice cubes

Crack open the cardamom pods, empty their seeds into a small bowl, and toss in the pods. Add the saffron threads and boiling water. Stir well and let stand until the liquid has cooled to room temperature, about 15 minutes.

With a fork, remove the cardamom pods from the water and discard, leaving the seeds in the water. Place the cardamom-saffron water, yogurt, coconut milk, and agave nectar in a blender and process for 30 seconds to mix well.

Immediately before serving, add the ice to the blender and puree until smooth and frothy, about 1 minute. Taste for sweetness and add more agave nectar if you like. Serve in 2 tall, slender glasses, garnishing each with a pinch of saffron.

Yield: 2 servings

# Asparagus and Sweet Potato Curry

*This curry features a zesty sauce in which paper-thin slices of sweet potatoes are simmered until meltingly tender, along with oven-roasted asparagus. Bryant says, "Because asparagus spears, like most vegetables, start losing nutrients and flavor immediately after they are harvested, buy them at your nearest farmers' market when they make their grand appearance this year. Trust me, you don't want to miss out on one bit of the vitamin C, potassium, B vitamins, copper, vitamin A, iron, phosphorus, and zinc that those delicious tiny spears contain." If you want to make your own garam masala, combine $1/4$ teaspoon each of ground black pepper, garlic powder, ground ginger, and ground cardamom, with $1/2$ teaspoon each of tumeric and ground cumin.*

Coarse sea salt
2 bunches of asparagus, trimmed
2 teaspoons plus 3 tablespoons coconut oil
$1/2$ teaspoon yellow mustard seeds
1 yellow onion, diced finely
3 cloves garlic, minced
1 teaspoon minced fresh ginger
2 teaspoons garam masala
$1/2$ teaspoons chili powder
1 teaspoon turmeric
2 bay leaves
1 (14-ounce) can diced tomatoes
1 (14-ounce) can coconut milk
1 large or 2 small sweet potatoes, peeled and
    thinly sliced
Freshly ground black pepper

Preheat the oven to 400°F.

In a large pot over high heat, bring 4 quarts of water to a boil. Add 1 tablespoon of salt, boil for 1 minute, then add the asparagus and immediately turn off the heat. Let sit for 1 minute, then drain.

Transfer the asparagus to a large plate and toss with the 2 teaspoons of coconut oil to coat lightly. Transfer the asparagus to a large baking sheet and roast until it starts to crisp, 8 to 10 minutes. Remove from the oven, cut diagonally into 1-inch pieces, and set aside.

In a large sauté pan over medium heat, warm the 3 tablespoons oil. Add the mustard seeds and cook until they pop, 2 to 3 minutes. Next, add the onion and sauté for 5 to 7 minutes, until soft and translucent. Then add the garlic, ginger, garam masala, chili powder, turmeric, bay leaves, and 1 teaspoon salt and sauté for an additional 2 minutes. Remove from the heat.

Put the tomatoes and their juices in a large bowl. With clean hands, squeeze the tomatoes through your fingers to break them into smaller pieces. Transfer the tomatoes to the sauté pan with the onions. Add the coconut milk, then fill the coconut milk can 1/4 full with water and stir it well to incorporate any coconut milk that may have been left behind. Add this to the sauté pan and mix well. Add the sweet potatoes and simmer over low heat for about 20 minutes, until they are tender and the sauce has thickened up. Add the asparagus, cover, and simmer for 1 minute. Remove from the heat.

Season with salt and pepper to taste and serve immediately. There will be plenty for seconds.

Yield: 4 to 6 servings

# Simple Yellow Rice

*Bryant says it's best to soak rice in water overnight. It makes it more digestible and shortens the cooking time. Unlike with beans, you can cook grains in the same water in which they are soaked.*

1 cup short-grain brown rice, soaked in water overnight
1 tablespoon extra-virgin olive oil
1 cup diced yellow onion
1 teaspoon turmeric
Coarse sea salt
$2^{1}/_{4}$ cups water

Drain the rice, saving the water if you like.

In a medium saucepan over low heat, combine the olive oil, onion, and salt and sauté until well caramelized, 10 to 15 minutes. Add the turmeric and stir until well incorporated, about 30 seconds. Add the rice and cook for about 2 minutes, stirring often, until any liquid has evaporated and the rice start to smell nutty.

Stir in $2^{1}/_{4}$ cups of water and bring to a boil over high heat. Cover, turn down the heat to low, and cook for 50 minutes.

Remove from the heat, but keep the lid on for at least 10 minutes to steam. Fluff the rice with a fork before serving. There will be plenty for seconds.

Yield: 4 servings

# Morning-After Breakfast:
## Creamy Oats with a Crunch

*You got lucky. Here's what Bryant says you should serve her for breakfast in bed. (The arginine-rich oatmeal and walnuts do wonders for your sexual health.) If you think you've got a sure thing, you can take Bryant's advice to soak the steel-cut oats overnight, but the dish can be thrown together in a pinch, using instant oats, if necessary.*

$1/2$ teaspoon ground cinnamon
1 tablespoon plus $1/2$ cup water
$1/2$ cup steel-cut oats
$1 1/2$ cups rice milk
$1/8$ teaspoon fine sea salt
$1/4$ teaspoon coconut oil
$1/4$ cup golden raisins
$1/2$ cup walnuts, toasted and chopped
1 tablespoons pure maple syrup

In a small bowl, combine the cinnamon with the 1 tablespoon of water and stir until well combined. In a medium saucepan, combine the cinnamon slurry with the remaining water, oats, rice milk, and salt. Swish around, cover, and refrigerate for 6 hours, or overnight if possible.

Over medium-low heat, bring the oats to a boil. Add the coconut oil and cook, stirring constantly, until the oats start to thicken, about 2 to 3 minutes. Immediately turn down the heat to low and simmer, uncovered, for 20 minutes, stirring often to prevent the mixture from sticking to the bottom of the pan.

Add the raisins and simmer for an additional 5 minutes. Remove from the heat and stir in the walnuts and maple syrup. Let stand for 5 minutes, then serve.

Yield: 2 servings

## Ooh, Baby: A Seductive Dessert from BabyCakes NYC

BabyCakes NYC is the sexiest little vegan bakery around. Its coveted cakes seem terribly decadent, but they're far healthier than they taste. Bake these brownies the afternoon before your date, while you're getting ready. Even if you don't get lucky, you won't mind eating them alone. Chocolate is the aphrodisiac that keeps on giving, because its heart-healthy, relaxation-inducing, antioxidant-rich properties are nice even when you're loverless.

### Agave-Sweetened Brownie Gems

*Be sure to keep a special eye on the agave with this recipe. It'll dictate whether you end up with a dry chocolate roll or a luscious fudgelike brownie.*

$^1/_2$ cup garbanzo–fava bean flour
$^1/_4$ cup brown rice flour
$^1/_4$ cup potato starch
2 tablespoons arrowroot powder
$^1/_2$ cup unsweetened cocoa powder
2 teaspoons baking powder
$^1/_4$ teaspoon baking soda
$^1/_4$ teaspoon xanthan gum
1 teaspoon salt

$^1/_2$ cup coconut oil, plus more for the tins

$^1/_3$ cup agave nectar

$^1/_2$ cup homemade applesauce or store-bought
unsweetened applesauce

1 tablespoon pure vanilla extract

$^1/_2$ cup hot water or hot coffee

Preheat the oven to 325°F. Lightly grease three 12-cup mini-muffin tins with oil.

In a medium bowl, whisk together the flours, potato starch, arrowroot, cocoa powder, baking powder, baking soda, xanthan gum, and salt. Add the $^1/_2$ cup oil and the agave nectar, applesauce, vanilla, and hot water to the dry ingredients and stir until the batter is smooth.

Using a melon baller, scoop the batter into each prepared mini-muffin cup. Bake the brownies on the center rack for 9 minutes, rotating the tins 180 degrees after 5 minutes. (For a more fudgy-tasting cake, bake for only 8 minutes total.) The finished brownies will have firm edges with a soft center, and a toothpick inserted in the center will come out clean.

Let the brownies stand in the tins for 20 minutes, or until completely cool. To maintain freshness, leave the brownies in the muffin tins until ready to serve. Cover with plastic wrap and store at room temperature for up to 3 days.

Yield: 36 cupcakes

*Reprinted with permission from* BabyCakes: Vegan, (Mostly) Gluten-Free, and (Mostly) Sugar-Free Recipes from New York's Most Talked-About Bakery, *by Erin McKenna, published by Clarkson Potter, 2009.*

# Eco-Cooking:
## Tips and Tools of the Trade

Cooking should be not just a utilitarian task—it should be a seductive adventure. There are many excellent tools available to help you keep everything eco-friendly while you're cooking up a love storm.

Cook more than one item at a time. One-pot cooking reduces energy consumption. Cut your food into smaller pieces before you heat it, thus shortening the cooking time for denser foods. Buy cookware with tight-fitting lids and use them—this speeds up cooking time and saves energy.

Avoid Teflon, which emits toxic gases, and aluminum, linked to Alzheimer's disease and other illnesses. Even stainless steel, thought by many to be a safer alternative, contains chromium and nickel. Since we don't know how much these heavy metals and chemicals leach into our food at high heat, it's best to go with something safer. Greenpots (greencookingpots.com) makes enameled cast-iron pots free of chemicals. The pots absorb heat and evenly distribute it, making cooking faster and more efficient.

# More Aphrodisiac Eco-Foods

Seek out organic, fair-trade, and locally grown versions of the following foods and herbs.

**Asparagus:** The suggestive form isn't the whole story. These sexy stalks are rich in vitamin E, something you need lots of.

**Chile peppers:** Capsaicin is a chemical that stimulates nerve endings and makes us sweat. Hot peppers stimulate the body to release endorphins.

**Chocolate:** This confection can't be mentioned too often. Beyond its heavenly taste, it contains phenylethylamine, known as the "love chemical." Chocolate officially makes you high.

**Damiana:** This is better known as wild yam. It's thought to stimulate female hormones and cause erotic dreams when consumed before bed.

**Oysters:** Oysters are full of zinc, a precursor to testosterone. Some also think they look like female genitalia, and Casanova himself was known to eat them in great quantities before sex. If you can find sustainably sourced oysters, see what they do for you.

# Serving Up Seduction

The classic dinner date is an institution, but the eco-sexual options for dining out are still evolving. Jared Koch is the founder of Clean Plates New York (cleanplatesnyc.com), an organization with a nutritionist- and food-critic-approved guidebook to the tastiest, healthiest restaurants in Manhattan (with many more cities on tap). Jared is a nutritional consultant and a foodie all wrapped in one. He suggests looking for restaurants that are concerned with more than price when it comes to sourcing their ingredients. Don't be afraid to restaurant shop. Call and ask questions; don't worry about coming off like Meg Ryan's character in *When Harry Met Sally*, ordering a salad with dressing on the side. For restaurants that serve animal foods, Clean Plates's minimum requirement is that they be hormone and antibiotic free. Beyond that, Koch suggests looking for pasture-raised, grass-fed, free-range, organic, and locally raised animals. Local, organic produce is an important consideration, as is the quality of oils, salts, and sweeteners the restaurant uses. Clean Plates also pays close attention to how many veggies are on the menu and looks for gluten-free, vegan, or at least vegetarian options.

If you do have access to vegan and vegetarian joints, Jared suggests you try to find places that are using real, whole foods and a minimal amount of fake soy and seitan. Consider whether or not the restaurant filters their water—don't be afraid to ask. Do they serve biodynamic or organic wines and other alcohol? Fair-trade and organic coffee and tea? Finally, opt for restaurants that offer naturally sweetened desserts as well as gluten-free and dairy-free options.

"A lot of restaurants don't choose to promote the fact that they use more sustainable ingredients," reveals Jared. So again, the rule of thumb is to call in advance and ask.

# Accompaniment: Eco-Wining with Your Dining

Getting sustainable, eco-friendly wine onto the tables of foodies hasn't been an easy task. There is a lot of greenwashing in this industry, and regulators are only slowly catching up with it. Organic wine labeling is a decidedly confusing topic. In order for a wine to be certified USDA organic, it has to be free of sulfites. It must also be "made with organic grapes." The rules are less strict here, but the winery still needs to incorporate organic standards. Biodynamic wine is made using biodynamic agriculture, a form of organic farming that sees the farm as a self-contained entity with its own individuality. Nutrients are recycled and composting is emphasized.

Jung Kim, wine expert and owner of Piermont Wines of New York, recommends the following eco-friendly vintages:

- Cakebread Cabernet Sauvignon
- Frog's Leap Merlot
- Saintsbury Pinot Noir
- Hall Sauvignon Blanc
- Schramsberg Blanc de Blancs or Blanc de Noirs Champagne

Jung also likes a few other eco-friendly wineries, including Bonny Doon Vineyards (bonnydoonvineyard.com), Calera Vineyards (calera wine.com), and Quivira Vineyards (quivirawine.com).

# That's the Spirit

Want something a little harder? If you prefer liquor to wine, you also have some green options.

- Rain Organic Vodka comes in a variety of fun flavors.
- Square One Vodka is distilled from organically grown North Dakota rye, and the bottles are unfrosted (frosting requires a harsher chemical process).
- Juniper Green organic gin is made from organic grains and herbs.
- Papagayo Organic Rum is made from organically farmed sugarcane grown ethically in Paraguay.

Sated yet? If not, in the next chapter you can satisfy your appetite for chocolate, roses, and baubles without harming the earth or the people who share it with you.

# CHAPTER FIVE

# Are Diamonds (and Chocolate and Roses) Really a Girl's Best Friend? Giving the Gift of Love Responsibly

When you're hungry for love you'll go to great lengths to court your intended, spending a lot of money, dressing to impress, and pouring time and energy into various creative wooing technologies. This chapter covers the ultratraditional means of courtship: flowers, chocolate, and jewelry.

## Don't Bring Me (Unsustainable) Flowers Anymore

A rose by any other name may smell as sweet, but when it's brought to your lover's door by air freight from mammoth plantations in Ecuador and Colombia, it's pretty foul indeed. Many of the underpaid laborers in these flower farms are children, prized for their small hands. And behind a dozen delicate roses lurks a poisonous health hazard—pesticides. Yet if you love to give or get gorgeous, great-smelling petaled lovelies, you don't have to go wanting. The greenest option is to grow your own organic flowers in your yard and cut them yourself for the one you want to woo. If you don't have the space, call around and see if any of your local florists sell organic, locally grown blooms. Try your local farmers' market too. Localharvest.org will help you find flowers by zip code if you don't have luck with the yellow pages. If you shop at Trader Joe's, Safeway, Whole Foods, or Costco, you can often find fair-trade flowers certified by VeriFlora or the Rainforest Alliance. Look carefully at labels and ask the manager of your local store what they sell. If they don't stock fair-trade flowers, ask them to start.

Farmers' market flowers are usually the greenest. They're often in the Asteraceae family (zinnias, dahlias, coneflowers, daisies, black-eyed Susans, sunflowers, asters, and cosmos). The least green are those we import, not only because of the energy costs to ship them, but also because by nature they are more tender and more difficult to grow, require more water, or require more energy.

Of all the flowers in the United States, 80 percent are imported, usually from Ecuador and Colombia. The top five imported flowers in the United States are roses, gerberas, carnations (it should be noted that dianthus, the earlier wild versions of carnations, are very easy to grow organically), chrysanthemums (also of the Asteraceae family, but these are the show kind, as opposed to the hardy garden variety, and they require more care and energy), and tulips (considered easy to care for and grow, but seasonal unless "forced," the practice of refrigerating bulbs to trick them into thinking they've wintered).

If you don't have success with local vendors, try Organic Bouquet (organicbouquet.com), an online flower delivery service that has a carbon-offset program and uses eco-packaging. Or try FiftyFlowers .com, which will send you wholesale rose petals overnight. However, this can be a bit much unless you're planning a wedding or have lots of friends to whom to give the extra petals as gifts. Other options are California Organic Flowers, Diamond Organics, or local organic florists such as Gardenia Organic in New York City. There's likely to be one just like it in your town; if not, tell local florists that you want them to carry the good stuff.

## Flower Certification Options

- Biodynamic
- Certified organic (USDA)
- Ecocert
- Fair-trade certified
- FlorEcuador certification
- Florverde
- Rainforest Alliance
- VeriFlora

# Chocolate-Flavored Love: Keep My Cocoa Handy

Do you have a sweet tooth when it comes to love? Chocolate is a psychoactive food made from the tropical cacao tree, *Theobroma cacao*, a Latin name that loosely translates to "food of the gods" in Greek. The Aztecs first made a hot beverage out of cacao beans that was served solely to priests, noblemen, and warriors. Casanova famously ate chocolate before bedding his many conquests. Chocolate is so entrenched in the lore of lovers that it's almost a cliché. But it shouldn't be, because its effects on libido aren't an old wives' tale. Of course, anything delicious gets our pleasure sensors buzzing, and that makes us want a little sumthin' sumthin'. But it's also high in arginine, a substance linked to sexual potency (for more on this substance, see chapter 6, "Sexual Healing"). Dark chocolate has also been found to be good for the heart—its flavonols are believed to help lower blood pressure and can reduce cardiovascular diseases. Chocolate contains over three hundred chemical substances, including phenylethylamine, caffeine, and theobromine, another stimulant. The neurotransmitters released after eating chocolate (the chocolate "high") might be the reason chocolate lovers are thought to have better sex lives, according to a 2004 Italian study.[20]

But—and it's a big *but*—not all chocolate meets an eco-sexual's high standards. The chocolate industry is known for breaches of ethics, like unsafe working conditions, below-poverty wages, and child slavery. All chocolate is not alike, so before you take another bite, find out where yours comes from.

The Ivory Coast, the world's largest cocoa producer, produces 43 percent of the world's chocolate, and two U.S. companies control two-thirds of the $13 billion U.S. chocolate candy market. The International Labor Rights Fund filed a lawsuit against Nestlé on behalf of Malian children trafficked to the Ivory Coast in 2005. Although the chocolate industry agreed to begin self-regulating around this time (thanks to congressional pressure), little has happened since. Nestlé says that they're just the buyers of the product and can't control what happens on the ground in Africa. That kind of excuse isn't acceptable for a chocolate-hungry eco-sexual. Look for third-party-certified fair-trade labels, or find the following brands online or in stores.

**Dagoba:** The company may have been bought out by Hershey's, but it's still the real deal. Dagoba sources from five different countries, from either fair-trade co-ops or small farmers with whom they work out agreements similar to fair-trade arrangements (workers get 1.5 times the minimum wage, health care, reasonable work hours and expectations, and so on). In each country, it appears that the company contributes to the social and ecological health of the surrounding area in important ways. In Costa Rica and Peru, the company helps women's co-ops. In Costa Rica, representatives also work with a neighboring preserve to track the health of the sloth. In all locations, the farming is organic and sustainable, which is extremely important because of the deforestation that often results from cacao farming.

Dagoba seeks to source just one varietal for each product, in order to bring the unique flavor of that single varietal to the finished chocolate—an unusual practice in the industry. The founder is a former chef, so he has chosen his sources for their distinctive qualities. This focus on single varietals, often heirlooms, is important especially in Ecuador, where so much cross-pollination has occurred that an important varietal (the one Dagoba uses) is on the verge of extinction. In helping to providing a market for the pure heirloom, Dagoba is helping it to survive.

The leaders at Dagoba package with recycled paper and pay 20 percent more for their energy so that it comes from alternative energy sources (the EPA gave them a Green Power Leadership Award). And they're a member of the World Cacao Foundation, which works with the Bill and Melinda Gates Foundation to make cacao sustainable. The ingredients are certified organic—including the sugar, essential oils, and nuts, where available.

**TCHO:** TCHO's "thing" is technology. Its founder is an ex-NASA guy who worked on space shuttles, and the other major player is the founder of *Wired* magazine. These guys took a chocolate making machine and analyzed what it does at every juncture, perfecting it with the help of a roboticist. The company reinvests proceeds to buy, on behalf of farmers, drying and fermenting equipment that the farmers can't afford, in order to improve quality (this equipment might cost $300, which is what a farmer might make from an entire year's crop). This enables the farmers they work with to sell their beans at a premium and sets them above the mass market. This is essentially creating fair-trade conditions, but without creating co-ops. TCHO uses fair-trade-certified cocoa beans where available. But the company found that co-op creation is not always an option, such as on large plantations, and for small farmers in Ghana who sell to a national cocoa board. Such reinvestment in education and technology for farmers of cocoa is unusual. TCHO also explicitly states its opposition to slavery—company officials want to make it known that about a third of all cocoa produced in the world may be made through child slavery (given that a third comes from Ivory Coast, which continues to be rife with this inhumane practice).

TCHO uses organic beans in three of its four flavors. One of its flavors is 100 percent organic, while another product is moving toward being 100 percent organic and fair trade. See if you can't get a potential lover to follow you home by dropping a trail of their insanely decadent dried mango morsels (dipped in dark chocolate), *ET*-style.

**Denman Island:** This company is small and family owned. I found a rave review on a blog by a woman who loved the chocolate so much that she asked to visit the factory, and she was invited to stay overnight in their home for her tour. These chocolate bars are both delicious and beautifully packaged—they make a lovely gift for your intended.

The chocolate bars are 100 percent organic, including all added ingredients. The added coffee is from fairly traded Latin American beans. The factory is a big, gorgeous house (really!) on Denman Island, British Columbia. It's made with recycled fir boards and Paperstone, uses a wood stove for heat in the winter, and needs no air-conditioning in the summer. The melter inside is a "cozy" that saves energy. And the forestland surrounding the factory is under perpetual covenant so it will always be preserved. The company donates 1 percent of its profits to conservation societies. The added ingredients seem to mostly be local.

**Art Bar:** Art Bar makes some damn good chocolate without emulsifiers or soy. The bars are 100 percent organic—which includes all of the ingredients, not just the chocolate. They're also vegan and fair-trade certified. All paper used has recycled content. And 10 percent of profits go to art education. Art Bar was started by an art historian who wanted to give contemporary artists more exposure. Instead of opening a gallery she created Art Bars. Information about energy use at the factory is not publicly available, but given the company's support for organic farming and fair-trade practices, and how much it gives to charity, Art Bar has got plenty going for it in the admirable department.

**Vosges:** This elegant line of chocolate is also eco-friendly and is making a real effort not only to have an organic line but to move the entire company in a truly green direction. The factory and all boutiques run on 100 percent wind power. The company's use of recycled papers for packaging and shipping is impressive. Their processes incorporate water- and soy-based inks wherever possible. The packaging is purple and attractive and useful for repurposing, so employees work with an organization that gives leftover and excess packaging materials to art educators in Chicago. Printer cartridges and any old computers are also recycled. Any plastic used is polylactic acid (biodegradable), including the air-bag cushions used for shipping. The organic chocolate is from the Dominican Republic and is Rainforest Alliance Certified (as well as Oregon Tilth and USDA organic certified), and this means the company pays fair wages to producers.

**Newman's Own Organics:** With both the USDA organic and Rainforest Alliance seals, this down-to-earth chocolate line has got great eco street cred. The Espresso Dark Chocolate bar is a lovely treat after an afternoon delight. The chocolate peanut butter cups are decadent desserts unto themselves; you need only one.

# Ecologically Responsible Jewelry

Jewelry is the stickiest wicket when it comes to responsible giving. Leonardo DiCaprio certainly brought a wave of attention to the "blood diamond" industry a few years ago, but sadly the problem is still far from resolved. It's challenging to stay on the right side of this complex ethical issue.

## Diamonds: Still Not a Girl's Best Friend

Back in 2000, when the horrors of the diamond mining industry were coming to light, representatives in the industry made a rather fruitless attempt at self-regulation after the United Nations called them out on their abuses. This industry-approved policing mechanism, called the Kimberly Process, addresses only nations in an official state of civil conflict. It ignores labor, environmental, and human rights abuses. As of 2007, both Amnesty International and Global Witness believed that the industry wasn't doing enough to ensure that gems were ethically mined. There is still no such thing as a truly conflict-free diamond. The mining world is, in reality, not able to produce gems or precious metals that don't have serious social, political, or environmental consequences. Another complication, however, is that green consumers (that's you, Mr. or Ms. Eco-Sexual) can sometimes end up hurting the small-scale, artisanal mining operations that employ thirteen million poor people in Africa; avoiding purchasing any mined gems or metals at all inadvertently detracts from the livelihood of desperately poor people. This is why doing your homework is so important. The Kimberly Process could very well evolve into a mechanism that is a true measure of a gem's conflict-free and eco-friendly status, but there is a ways to go before this happens. Happily, if you're a gem-lovin' gal, you can try some of the nice alternatives listed later in this chapter.

## Good as Gold

All that glitters may not be gold, but even worse is the mercury that is used in the mining of real gold. Thousands of mining sites in Africa, Latin America, and Asia use as much as 1,000 tons of mercury a year. This poisonous element destroys the nervous systems of the workers and then leaches into oceans and riverbeds, contaminating fish and eventually getting onto our plates and into our bodies. Unregulated small-scale gold mining is nearly the worst source of mercury pollution in the world, second only to the mining of fossil fuels. Mercury is also sold on a dangerous black market. Indeed, conflict-gold is the new conflict-diamond. Gold is funding a war in the Democratic Republic of Congo that, as of 2009, has killed more than five million people.[21] The workers in the Congolese gold mines are desperate and destitute. Is that conventional gold necklace really worth contributing to all that war, pollution, and strife?

## Eco-Sexy Bling

Planning to woo your intended with some bling? Let the retailer know that you'll only buy gems and metals sourced from ethical mines that don't harm their workers or the environment. Ask for documentation and third-party certification. You may encounter literature from trade associations like the Jewelers of America. But keep in mind that groups like this don't necessarily exist to protect those who suffer the worst effects of the mining industries; they exist to protect the bottom line of retailers. Be sure to research companies thoroughly before dropping into the store. As of 2009, Walmart, the biggest seller of gold in the United States, said they will trace their gold back to its source, but only for 10 percent of the gold they sell. You should only trust those purveyors that can trace all of their gems or gold to the source. (Tiffany & Co., incidentally, is one of the few retailers that does so. All of their gold comes from a mine in Utah.) If you're going the synthetic route, don't assume that your gems are clean and green. Ask questions and request to see documentation on these products as well. You can learn more about what to look for—and avoid—at NoDirtyGold.org.

GreenKarat.com sets the gold standard (pardon the pun) for finding precious metals and gems in jewelry form. They suggest that you buy only recycled or secondhand gold, natural diamonds, or other gems. When looking at human-made gems, make sure they are cut in factories with fair conditions for workers.

Because conditions continue to evolve, use the following resources to make your own informed decision.

- Alliance for Responsible Mining: communitymining.org
- CAFOD: cafod.org.uk
- Earthworks: earthworksaction.org
- Fair Trade Jewelry: fairjewelry.org
- Global Witness: globalwitness.org
- Green America (formerly Co-op America): greenamericatoday.org
- Oxfam: oxfam.org
- World Wildlife Fund (WWF): worldwildlife.org

The following are some ethical, eco-friendly jewelers and costume-jewelry makers.

- The Andean Collection: theandeancollection.com
- April Doubleday: aprildoubleday.com
- CRED: credjewellery.com
- Dawes Design: dawes-design.com
- Dirty Librarian Chains: dirtylibrarianchains.com
- Fair Trade Gems: fairtradegems.com
- Fifi Bijoux: fifibijoux.com
- Hoover & Strong: hooverandstrong.com
- Kumvana Gomani: kumvanagomani.com
- Sumiche Jewelry: sumiche.com
- URTH: urthjewellery.com

You've got your eco-bling, your chocolate, and a vase of lovely flowers. What comes next? Get your health on, eco-sexual.

PART II

# THE NUTS AND THE BOLTS OF THE BIRDS AND THE BEES: ECO-SEX IS HEALTHY SEX

# sexual Healing, or Big Pharma vs. your Big O: How naturally Healthy lovers ditch the little Blue Pill in favor of green

Research shows that the healthier we are, the better our sex lives will be. And the opposite is true: if we're sluggish, sick, and struggling to get through an average day, forget about having a satisfying sex life. A romp in the hay is your lowest priority when you're exhausted and unwell. But here's the down and dirty truth: sex can in fact *make* you well. Sex boosts chemicals in the body that protect against disease. So hurry up and eat your organic vegetables—and keep on getting busy—you little eco-sexual, you.

First a little Disease Prevention 101. Much of what we understand to be "sickness" is merely a result of a toxic soup of industrial chemicals in our food, water, and air. And when this results in sexual dysfunction, a closed loop of self-doubt and depression feeds into an already existing condition. People often think something is physically wrong with them if they can't get it up or can't get turned on. It turns out that, in a great majority of cases, changing your diet, your environment, and your stress level can rescue your sex life.

# Big Pharma: Sex, Drugs, and Rock 'n' Roll in your Senator's Hotel Room

In a world where Viagra commercials run every hour, it's hard to see past the messages churned out by Madison Avenue. Behind these ads is the ugly truth: Big Pharma spends an almost unimaginable amount of cash lobbying legislators, and corporate scruples remain alarmingly low. But all we see is the guy in a claw-foot bathtub holding hands with his wife, subtly concealing what we can only imagine is a huge, long-lasting erection. According to the Center for Public Integrity, Big Pharma doled out $855 million between 1998 and 2006—more than any other industry in the United States.[22] That's a far less romantic picture than the one painted by the commercial, isn't it?

Doctors are usually our first line of defense when things go wrong in the bedroom. The bad news is that a lot of them have been compromised by industry. It's not their fault—it's just the system. Those free pills they throw at you when you're wearing a paper robe are not necessarily shared out of openhearted generosity. Pharmaceutical reps give doctors samples in order to hook patients and build lifelong relationships (read: addictions) just like your street-corner drug pusher. There are also conflicts of interest in the medical ghostwriting arena, which can lead to the publishing of compromised science and then approval of the drugs being reported on. Drug companies also conduct and publish their own studies, and their masterful public relations teams often feed this information to the media. They're all in bed with each other, and this is one ugly orgy you definitely don't want to join. Needless to say, it's wise to be cautious and do your homework when considering any new drugs prescribed by your doctor.

## Music, Sweet Music

A 2008 study conducted by Dr. Michael Miller, director of preventative cardiology at the University of Maryland Medical Center in Baltimore, reported that blood vessel diameter improved when people listened to their favorite music. Dr. Carl Lavie, medical director of cardiac rehabilitation and prevention director of the Stress Testing Laboratory at the Ochsner Heart and Vascular Institute in New Orleans, said, "Although this was just an acute [short-term] study, it suggests that laughter and listening to relaxing music may provide cardio-protection or be heart-healthy."[23] Since blood flow is a key element in great sex, tune in and turn on.

Some musicians are greener than others, running their tour buses on biodiesel and only distributing their work via the Internet. The Green Music Alliance, formed in 2008, is a group of artists and music industry types invested in lowering their collective carbon footprint. Here's a partial list of earth-friendly bands and musicians:[24]

| | | |
|---|---|---|
| Barenaked Ladies | K. T. Tunstall | Serj Tankian |
| Bonnie Raitt | Missy Higgins | Sheryl Crow |
| Cloud Cult | Moby | The Roots |
| Green Day | Pearl Jam | Thom Yorke |
| Guster | Perry Farrell | (Radiohead) |
| Jack Johnson | Sarah Harmer | Willie Nelson |

# Nutrition: Eating for Your Orgasm

At this stage of our evolution, the typical Western diet is, in a word, disgusting. It's quite literally killing us slowly. Aside from the goods in the produce aisle, almost everything for sale at your local supermarket is processed to the point of being unrecognizable as food. Even when it comes to fruits and veggies, a plethora of dangers lurks in those bins, unless you can buy from a trusted organic, non-GMO source or pick from your own backyard garden. The government of Austria recently confirmed the results of previous studies that had found that GMOs, specifically genetically modified corn, can damage the reproductive system and lower fertility rates after consumption for as little as twenty weeks. Pesticides, herbicides, and genetically modified organisms are just a few of the scary substances you're liable to ingest if you're not careful (as we learned in chapter 3). Let's look at how nutritional issues can relate to sexual health.

## Say Yes to NO

Nitric oxide (NO) is a chemical messenger that our body relies on for much of its functioning. More specifically, both male and female organs engorge during arousal, and nitric oxide is vital for this feat of nature to take its course. This naughty and necessary chemical pumps our blood, rules our central nervous system and our brain, and is responsible for the health of the cardiovascular system. We produce natural NO when we exercise, but eating foods rich in L-arginine gets it pumping, because it converts to NO in your body. In order to keep your sex life in tip-top shape, work out like crazy and eat loads of the foods in the following list.

## Arginine-Rich Foods

| | | | |
|---|---|---|---|
| Almonds | Garlic | Peanuts | Sunflower seeds |
| Chickpeas | Ginseng | Root veggies | Tuna |
| Coconut | Green veggies | Salmon | Walnuts |
| Flaxseeds | Oatmeal | Soybeans | And, best of all, chocolate |

# Shake It, Don't Break It

*Sex without love is merely healthy exercise.*
—Robert Heinlein

Exercise. Some of us are addicted to it and some of us hate it. But if you want a healthy sex life, you'd better make friends with the treadmill. Statistics show that the endorphin rush from a sweaty workout can make us randier on the spot. You're more relaxed after a session, and you're likely to feel that you've done something to improve your waistline. Exercise is empowering because it makes us feel like we're more in control of our lives. That kind of power is an instant aphrodisiac.

## Yoga

Yoga has incredible physical benefits (flexibility; lubrication of joints, ligaments, and tendons; organ health; detoxification; muscle toning) and is also the perfect starting point for anyone suffering from physiologically or psychologically based sexual imbalance. Even without meditation, yoga helps you become more comfortable with your body by bringing you *beyond* the body. No matter what your perspective is on spirituality, yoga teaches awareness. It quiets the mind, teaches breathing, and helps you to focus on singular poses, or asanas, that in turn provide increased focus. Yoga also teaches you to master your physical energy, which can help you to control orgasm, making for longer-lasting sex sessions. And the flexibility that comes with yoga? Well, that goes without saying. The new positions you'll be able to achieve with enough practice will blow both of your minds. It also increases endurance.

According to Jacquie Noelle Greaux and Jennifer Langheld, authors of *Better Sex Through Yoga*, there are ten principles that any budding yogi or yogini needs to understand. The following are my summaries of their spot-on principles:

1. **Compassion:** If you practice it every day in small ways, you'll automatically increase your own compassion for yourself, your partner, and anyone you encounter on the street. This "pay it forward" understanding of karma can improve your sex life in myriad ways.

2. **Body of knowledge:** The workout will tone and shape you, and that's always a plus when wearing the clingy outfit you're hoping to woo him with. But the more important element here is that you'll learn life-changing lessons about your own body. The result? You'll be a better lover.

3. **Movement:** Learning subtle movements can increase your pleasure. The easy flow of a fast-paced Vinyasa class gets your blood circulating and may assist you in quickly changing positions in bed.

*continued*

4. **Grace under pressure:** Stress-reduction is a lovely benefit of sex, but if you're so clenched up that you can't relax enough to even get in the mood, you'll get nowhere fast. Yoga reduces stress and performance anxiety.

5. **Flex it up:** Flexibility? Enough said.

6. **Strength:** Yoga builds strength and a sensation of lightness, which is always fun when you want to throw or be thrown around in bed, even just a little bit. (Your yoga classmates might make excellent bedmates, since they may be more likely to match your strength and agility, move for move.)

7. **Awareness:** Sex is all about staying in the moment—it's not fun when you're thinking about your grocery list. Yoga is one of the best tools on the planet for learning awareness and presence of mind.

8. **True inner happiness:** Yoga teaches that happiness comes from within, and that all is one in the universe. You may not become enlightened just from practicing yoga, but the small bits of joy you'll uncover each day will in turn make you a more joyful, sexy, self-loving person that anyone would want to be naked with.

9. **Fake it 'til you make it:** As with sex, new students of yoga often aim for perfection. Some feel frustrated when they can't get into complicated poses early on in their practice. But yoga teaches that you should try the harder asanas any- way, and if you don't get it right the first time you'll get there eventually. Just try to remain in a state of joy and open- heartedness no matter what.

10. **Burning enthusiasm:** Yoga shows you how to use your energy intentionally, actively, and passionately. You'll figure out where your hot, fiery center lives and learn how to isolate and trigger it at will.

# Meet Dr. Kegel (Your New Best Friend)

So you're eating healthy and exercising. What's next? Kegel exercises strengthen the pelvic floor. Thank Dr. Arnold Kegel for providing you with a simple exercise that can vastly improve your erotic life. The muscles involved in Kegel exercises include those that are engaged during urination, bowel movements, sex, and childbirth. Pregnant women and those with incontinence are also encouraged to practice Kegel exercises. (I'll bet you didn't know that men can do them too.) As you can see, practicing Kegels helps you in more ways than one. They're extremely easy and can be done anywhere, even while sitting at your desk at the office (no one will be the wiser). While sitting or lying down, you simply contract the same muscles you would use to stop urinating in midflow. You will feel this contraction in your urethra and anus, not in your stomach or buttocks. If you feel the other muscles tightening, try again until you've got it right. Once you've gotten the hang of it, just squeeze for three seconds and release for three seconds, repeating ten to fifteen times each session (three sessions a day is ideal). You can also get a Kegel exerciser, which is essentially a vaginal barbell.

## Stretching the Limits

Pelvic stretching keeps you limber and ready for sex. You can do the following exercises on the floor or on the bed. (Doing them with your partner is heartily encouraged.)

### Pelvic Lifts

Lie on your back with knees bent and slightly apart. Keep your feet flat on the floor and your arms at your sides. Inhale, then clench your abdominals and butt, lifting your pelvis until your back is straight.

(This is not the right moment to arch your back, darling.) Hold for 10 seconds and breathe deeply through the nose. Exhale as you lower your body. Repeat.

### Pelvic Bounces

Lie on your back with knees bent and slightly apart. Face your palms up. As you inhale, lift your pelvis slightly off the ground (or bed, or what have you). As you exhale, allow your lower back to bounce slightly against the floor.

### The Butterfly

Again, lie on your back with knees bent, feet together and flat on the floor. Pull your feet in until they touch your butt. Then turn your ankles so the soles of your feet are facing each other and touching. Your knees will point out to the side. Next, lower your knees toward the bed, making sure not to push them down with too much force. With your hands, you can softly press downward on your inner thighs (or your partner can do this). When your knees are as far apart

## Get Out of Your Head and Into the Heat of the Moment

Any exercise that lifts the veil between mind and body is one that's great for your sex life. Daily or weekly mindfulness meditation helps us to be in the moment when we find ourselves in a sexual situation. Meditation can also help you learn to control those annoying neurotic, niggling thoughts that creep in against your will, whether you're in bed or walking to work.

as they can reasonably go, hold the position for sixty seconds. Slowly bring your knees back together with your hands, breathe, and say, "ah." Alternatively, the butterfly can also be done sitting up, with a special friend. Sit back to back, with your spines pressed against one another. Soften your shoulders and try to keep your head in line with your spine. Move your feet in as close to your body as you can and turn them so your soles touch and knees point out. Hold your feet together. Then breathe deeply and lower your knees gently, making sure not to use too much force. The butterfly helps with menstrual and urinary problems and may ease the stress of childbirth—if you forgot to use birth control, that is.

# Societal Conditioning

Tens of millions of American men regularly use Viagra, Cialis, and Levitra. But there are safer, healthier ways for guys to get it up. You can avoid awkward moments in the bedroom (and trips to the pharmacy) without risking the side effects of pharmaceutical drugs. How? By living clean, which means removing toxins from the body through good nutrition, elimination of alcohol and tobacco, and stress reduction. Daily exercise also improves general health and helps reduce impotence. When stress is a factor, herbs like Saint-John's-wort and kava kava are far less dangerous remedies than prescription medication.

Our society is slightly insane when it comes to its "penis problems," and the pharmaceutical industry has seized on this. Erectile dysfunction (ED) is the artist formerly known as "impotence," but that term was found to be offensive by the industry, so Big Pharma copywriters dreamed up a new one that better rolled off the tongue. ED sometimes has a psychological basis and is sometimes caused by physiological issues, but in both cases reaching for a pill can fail to address the cause.

Stress is common, and hormonal changes are inevitable, and they definitely affect the sex drive of both men and women. But Western medicine's understanding of cause and effect is quite similar to the thinking that got us into the environmental mess we're in. That classic American short-term thinking gives the execs of Big Pharma exponentially expanding McMansions, but it doesn't give you a healthy orgasm.

And ladies, just wait until BioSante Pharmaceuticals, a Big Pharma player, introduces LibiGel, a drug they're developing to treat low libido in women. Doctors may soon be slyly pushing packets of LibiGel when their women patients complain about feeling less than libidinous. Women should always look at diet, exercise, psychological issues, and environmental concerns before popping a pill or rubbing medicine onto their skin.

# New Paradigm, New Definitions

If we aspire to redefine sexual health for a new generation of eco-sexuals, we should start by redefining sexual "dysfunctions" or "conditions." Let's call them "imbalances," with the understanding that we can almost always bring our bodies back into balance with a combination of nutrition, detoxification, exercise, and psychological wellness. It's the pharmaceutical industry that wants you to believe that you're "dysfunctional" and therefore must rely on their wares. Before you fall for that line, explore your other options. Note: No information here should be used to diagnose or treat illness; always seek the advice of a qualified practitioner if you're not sure what's going on with your body. Holistic doctors, including homeopaths, herbalists, naturopaths, acupuncturists, and others are excellent choices when you're moving away from the traditional Western paradigm. But for diagnosis of serious conditions, there's no reason to shun your friendly neighborhood doctor.

## Sexual Imbalances in Women

Most of the time, stress and fatigue are the lifestyle issues that should be addressed first. Low sex drive, delayed or total absence of orgasm, and painful intercourse due to muscle spasms or insufficient lubrication are just a few of the sexual issues that can often be traced back to lifestyle.

Let's not ignore the elephant in the room: past sexual trauma or abuse can also cause psychological issues. Women generally need to feel safe and valued in a sexual partnership in order to get turned on. Mental stress can inhibit lubrication and sexual arousal, something doctors often find in female orgasmic disorder and female sexual arousal disorder. Psychological trauma can also create an association of pain with intimacy, which can lead to vaginismus, or the involuntary contraction of the vaginal muscles to the point that penetration is either impossible or exceptionally painful.

A deep understanding of one's own issues is an integral part of a healthy sex life. If you're uncomfortable with your sexuality for any reason, try to explore it with a therapist. Within the context of a relationship, the most important thing you can do is share your fears and ideas about pleasure with your partner. If you don't feel comfortable doing that, it'll be hard to fix what's broken. Safe, open communication is definitely essential in sexual partnerships.

## Toxins: What to Get Out of Your System Before You Put Anything In

While alcohol and certain drugs are definitely potential obstacles to sexual enjoyment (because they can tend to restrict proper blood flow to all parts of the body, sex organs included), what's lurking in your medicine cabinet may be even worse. Prescription medications are the secret villains in a lot of women's sexual imbalances. The most common are antidepressants, antianxiety medicines, blood pressure medicines, and sedatives, all of which can lower blood pressure and affect proper blood flow to the genitalia. If you have sexual issues, avoid antihistamines, which dry out the vagina just as they can dry out a stuffy nose. (For sinus issues, try a Neti Pot instead of the over-the-counter pharmaceutical approach. And for hay fever and allergies, check out nettle root extract.) Birth control pills can affect sexual satisfaction and inhibit arousal and have been linked to hypoactive sexual disorder in women. (This topic is discussed in more detail in chapter 7.)

## Physical Conditions: Pelvic Floor Prolapse, Urinary Tract Infections, Allergies, and Other Maladies

The culprits of female sexual imbalances abound. Pelvic floor prolapse occurs when the muscles that support the pelvic organs are loosened because of childbirth, plain old aging, surgical procedures, or spinal cord injury. Diseases like diabetes, chronic fatigue, arthritis, multiple sclerosis, and cardiovascular disease are also cited as causes of inhibited sexual stimulation, because often the body is focused solely on survival, not reproduction and procreation.

Other culprits can lead to painful, less-than-fun sex. Urinary tract infections, yeast infections, and bladder infections can all cause pain in the genital region, which can in turn be linked to disorders related to painful spasms of the vaginal muscles, such as vaginismus and dyspareunia. (Dyspareunia is a fancy word for painful intercourse, which can also have psychological causes.) Allergic reactions to lotions, clothing fabrics, lubes, condoms, and other items can create painful sensations as well, but going green can help you avoid many of these. Because of the possibility of serious conditions such as cysts, endometriosis, tumors, or sexually transmitted diseases (STDs), women should consult their physicians if serious pain persists.

## Hormonal Changes and Menopause

Women's hormones fluctuate throughout their lives, starting before puberty and lasting pretty much forever. The dance of hormones is extremely complex, involving progesterone, estrogen, testosterone, and more. (Yes, women have testosterone in small amounts—it controls their sex drive just like it does in men.) Perimenopausal and premenopausal women can experience hormone fluctuations that sometimes interfere with arousal. Menopause, however, is seen as a leading contributing factor in many sexual disorders, as hormonal imbalances are often at their peak and the vaginal walls begin to thin during this time, potentially causing painful sex and sometimes a lowered desire for sexual activity. Of course, there are plenty of cougars around who would say this is bunk; their sex lives are just fine, thank you very much. And, because Big Pharma sees menopause as a disease, they're all over it, ready to dispense pills that you can pop to make it all go away. You so don't need to go there; there are plenty of natural ways to deal with the "change of life."

### Some Solutions Your Doctor Might Not Know About

Despite the issues relating to Big Pharma, your doctor is still your first line of defense and source of accurate diagnosis, so any concerns should be brought to his or her office. But if prescriptions are suggested, check into herbal alternatives first. Black cohosh, chaste tree, damiana, dandelion, false unicorn root, ginkgo, ginseng, licorice, life root, raspberry, red clover, sage, Saint-John's-wort, sarsaparilla, saw palmetto, shepherd's purse, true unicorn root, and wild yam are some herbs than can prove helpful during menopause and in the years prior to it. Gotu kola can help improve circulation to the genital area. Coenzyme Q10 helps alleviate mental stress and fatigue. Valerian root is a nice sedative, while licorice and passionflower herb and extract can help ease feelings of sexual tension. And pelvic floor prolapse responds well to Kegel exercises. (If you don't have an herbalist to consult, check out *The Green Pharmacy Herbal Handbook*, by James A. Duke, for dosage guidance and information about contraindications.)

## Sexual Imbalances in Men

Problems with getting it up, keeping it up, and premature ejaculation are just a few issues guys deal with. Why on god's green earth would you have to suffer such madness? Stress, unbalanced diet, lack of exercise, and dysfunction of the liver, kidneys, and endocrine system are just a few unfortunate things that cause low testosterone levels. When testosterone is low, the sex drive is also generally low and can result in disorders like inhibited ejaculation (or anorgasmia). Too many toxins can also lead to imbalanced thyroxine and prolactin levels, which can also lead to inhibited ejaculation. So exercise, eat your veggies, and deal with your feelings if you want to keep pleasing your lover.

On the other hand, too much testosterone can be equally problematic. Testosterone levels can be exceptionally high in men if they are experiencing an enlarged prostate, have used steroids, have built excess muscle, or even have masturbated too frequently. (Sorry, boys.) High testosterone levels can also lead to premature ejaculation. Most agree that ejaculation within 90 seconds into a session would qualify as "too soon."

Nervous system health is integral to healthy sexuality. Nervous system damage as a result of diabetes, multiple sclerosis, or stroke can cause inhibited ejaculation. Injury to the penis or groin can also cause Peyronie's disease, a curvature of the penis as it becomes erect because of the formation of hard, fibrous scar tissue underneath the skin or insufficient collagen production. That's why you wear a cup when you play sports, sir. Sex can be painful and embarrassing for guys in this situation. Surgeries on the prostate gland or urethra can result in the improper flow of semen (retrograde ejaculation). This condition is generally harmless; it's just a malfunction of the sphincter and a redirection of semen into the bladder. The less you think about it, the less it matters.

Hitting the sauce? Overconsumption of alcohol and drugs can have a negative impact as well, because proper circulation is just about the most important thing in healthy sexual function, and drinking or drugging can reduce circulation. Tobacco, caffeine, and prescription medications can cause the blood vessels to constrict and not allow for adequate flow to the penis. Just another good reason to live clean.

## Mind Over Matter

It's a myth that guys always want it and that women are the emotional ones. Guilt, anger, and fear can affect a man's level of sexual desire just as much as a woman's. Our intensely goal-oriented society can play a role as well. Men are incredibly stressed and under pressure to perform both at work and in the sack. For these reasons, communication is key for men in sexual relationships. Tell your partner what you want, how you want it, and why.

## The Carnal Cleanse

Cleansing is one of the keys to a healthy sex life. Arul Goldman, the owner and founder of SanaVita (sanavita.org), a colonic hydrotherapy and healing spa in New York City, recommends a three-day fruit detox for those who want to kick-start their metabolism and reinvigorate their sex lives. (You can continue your fruit diet as long as you like—however, do it under the supervision of an experienced holistic health professional.) Organic and locally grown fruit can include any of the following: apples, avocados, bananas, blackberries, blueberries, grapefruit, oranges, papaya, pineapple, raspberries, strawberries, tomatoes, watermelon, or white grapes. Arul's cleanse was inspired by the work of Dr. Edward Group III, whose book *Health Begins in the Colon* offers simple at-home solutions for cleansing both your body (internally) and your external living environment.

The best part of this cleanse is that there are no limits. You're not starving because you can eat as much fruit as you like, in five meals throughout the day. The trick is that you can only eat one kind of fruit at a time—no mixing in one meal. For example, eat only melon or grapefruit for breakfast. Or eat only oranges for your midmorning snack. Feel free to add lime juice or Himalayan salt crystals to any fruit for extra flavor and minerals. People tend to prefer to eat the tomatoes and avocadoes toward the evening, since they seem more like dinner foods. Don't eat anything after nine o'clock in the evening.

## Chronic Illness

Illnesses like hypertension, high blood pressure, heart disease, diabetes, chronic fatigue, and prostate problems can all inhibit a man's sexual abilities, primarily because of their effects on proper blood flow and nerve sensitivity. In general, chronic illnesses force the body

In addition to the fruit, your consume an intestinal cleansing beverage made from a concentrate of two ounces of organic apple cider vinegar, two ounces of organic aloe vera juice (whole leaf), and the juice of a lemon. You can sweeten this with yacon syrup to taste and add a teaspoon of vitamin C ascorbate powder for an extra kick. This concentrate should yield about five ounces of liquid. Add the concentrate to a gallon of pure water and consume the entire gallon throughout the day. (Many people like to fill an empty liter-sized bottle for portability; fill it about four times a day in order to consume the whole gallon.) For each of the three days, you will make a new gallon of the intestinal cleansing beverage.

In addition, take probiotics and digestive enzymes with every meal to get things moving (you get the drift). Arul recommends taking three Latero-Flora probiotic pills every morning between breakfast and the midmorning snack. Digestive enzymes will help to break down foods and improve absorption of nutrients overall. She suggests taking a plant-based physician-grade enzyme called Plantizyme. Take one or two with each meal. After the cleanse ends, you may want to continue with both the probiotics and the enzymes, because they're damn good for you.

Important note: It's crucial that you chew your food slowly and thoroughly. Do not eat quickly. As you chew, visualize all the benefits and nourishment you're getting from your food. And, of course, because this is a cleanse meant to improve your sex life, you can also imagine all the great sex you'll be having.

to focus more on basic survival than on procreation and, just as in women, this can lead to hypoactive sexual disorder. Health is sexual wealth, after all.

## Medication

We already learned about the dangers of a variety of prescription meds, but if you've been diagnosed with depression, take note: antidepressants can decrease sex drive by up to 60 percent in those who take them, because they suppress dopamine. Antipsychotics, antianxiety and blood pressure medications, sedatives, antihistamines, and decongestants can have negative effects on libido as well, particularly because of their effects on blood vessel function. WebMD cites more than sixty drugs that list erectile dysfunction as a side effect.[25]

## Other Physical Complications

One of the foremost causes of premature ejaculation is the unconscious oversensitization of the pelvic floor muscles, which are the muscles that sling below the abdominal organs and hold them in place. Pelvic floor muscles are involved in feelings of sexual pleasure,

## Horny Goat Weed—The New Viagra?

Researchers at the University of Milan tested horny goat weed and found it to be as effective as the little blue pill in treating erectile dysfunction, but with fewer side effects. The aptly named weed contains the compound icariin, which was isolated by the researchers and found to work as well as, and sometimes better than, Viagra. It's at least ten years away from being marketed as a pharmaceutical drug, but it is still available from your local herbalist.[26]

but when they're oversensitized by the frequent holding in of urine or flexing of the muscles during sex, they can present problems. Priapism, which occurs when blood gets trapped in the shaft of the penis, can be extremely painful and is not necessarily even a result of initial sexual stimulation.

## Solutions for Your Toolbox

Cellular health, and health of the whole body, is the key to a great sex life free of imbalance. Nutrition and cleansing are the first stop on a trip to a healthy sex life for guys. Taking B vitamins, zinc, magnesium, and potassium can help with disorders like retrograde ejaculation, and they can ease stress. For low sexual desire, passionflower extract, vitamin C, and weight training can help. Zinc, goldenseal, coenzyme Q10, supplements targeting vascular health, and even garlic and parsley can help those with erectile dysfunction. Yellow dock extract and supplements to aid prostate health may help those experiencing male anorgasmia as well as priapism. Men with premature ejaculation issues can find help from licorice, hawthorn berries, and relaxation techniques; masturbation is recommended three times a week at most. Even Peyronie's disease, which, of all those mentioned, seems like the most difficult to cure without pharmaceuticals or surgery, can be aided by the intake of vitamin E, vitamin C, quercetin, immune-boosting supplements, and magnesium and potassium. Again, it's wise to consult with your nutritionist, homeopath, naturopath, or whatever alternative doctor you fancy when taking a new course of vitamins or herbs.

Now that you're glowing from head to toe (and from the inside out), it's time to talk about protection. After all, babies are heavy-duty carbon emitters, and sexually transmitted diseases aren't fun either.

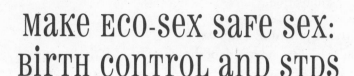

# chapter seven

# Make eco-sex safe sex: Birth control and STDs

Now that you've wooed and wined and dined your intended, you're ready to do the deed. But if you're part of a heterosexual couple of childbearing age, you've gotta deal with the fantasy-crushing subject of birth control. In a perfect world we could wish away potential pregnancy and sexually transmitted diseases and enjoy our lovemaking au natural. But our bodies, and the world we live in, make that impossible. So we have to do something about it. Before you run off to your doctor and get a prescription, let's look at what's wrong with traditional methods of birth control from the eco-sexual perspective.

## Avoiding Unwanted Pregnancy

In the most basic terms, in order to stop the sperm from making friends with the egg, you've got to block it from getting near the egg. This is usually done with a barrier method such as the condom, diaphragm, cervical cap, or, Elaine's favorite sexual companion, the sponge. (Remember *Seinfeld?*) If your guy is sponge-worthy, perhaps he's also willing to use an alternative, eco-friendly method of birth control. Remember that a lot of your comfort with various forms of birth control will depend on whether you're in a monogamous relationship and whether you and your partner have both been tested for STDs. Since we've established that unwanted children are very unfriendly to Mama Earth, find a method that's good for both of you.

## Condoms

According to *Slate* magazine, in 2008, 437 million condoms were sold, resulting in 2.75 million pounds of used-condom refuse in landfills nationwide.[27] Among American women, 18 percent favor condoms. Unfortunately, they have their flaws. Latex condoms are biodegradable, in theory, but before they turn back to compost they may spend a considerable number of years clogging landfills. The hardening agents and preservatives they're made with make this process quite slow. (Just make sure to avoid those made with polyurethane, an oil-derived material that does not biodegrade and brings us closer to the inevitability of peak oil.) Polyisoprene, a latex-like, thin, and stretchy material, is a great alternative for people with latex allergies. It's not "natural," but it does seem like promising technology. Lambskin condoms aren't a good eco-sexual choice for obvious reasons. Although they're biodegradable, they are made from cute little lambs, and they don't protect against STDs anyway. Most condoms are packaged in either plastic or tin wrapping (though when you buy in bulk you can at least recycle the box). If you want to create less waste, consider thinner condoms (not that you like thick condoms anyway). Most important, if you use condoms, don't flush them! They wreak more havoc in our waterways than they do in our landfills.

Wrap them in recycled tissue paper and throw them in the trash instead. Vegans will want to stick to Glyde condoms, a cruelty-free brand made without casein, a milk derivative common in condom manufacturing. Glyde's rubber is grown in Malaysia and the condoms are manufactured in Australia, for Aussie locavores. French Letter is the first condom company in the world to pay the fair-trade premium for latex rubber. The rubber plantation's workers are provided workers' benefits and appropriate wages to produce their biodegradable condoms.

By the time this book goes to press, another alternative might be available that will solve most of the problems that condoms currently have meeting eco-sexual standards. As of mid-2009, the company Yulex was planning to introduce a line of condoms with one of the major U.S. condom manufacturers. Yulex is a natural rubber latex derived from a desert shrub called guayule, which is grown in the desert of Arizona. Yulex latex is safe for the millions of individuals who suffer from type 1 latex allergy (tropical latex allergy). It's a biodegradable, renewable resource that might even have postproduction use as a biofuel. And because it's grown in the United States, the factory-to-market journey is shorter (for American eco-sexuals, at least). Visit Yulex's website (yulex.com) to find out where to get their condoms, dental dams, gloves, and other eco-sexual-friendly products.

## Neem Oil: Magic in a Bottle?

If the FDA ever gets around to testing it on humans, neem (*Azadirachta indica*), a fast-growing tree native to India, Pakistan, Myanmar, Bangladesh, and Sri Lanka, will change our sexual landscape. In India, the tree is variously known as "divine tree," "heal all," "nature's drugstore," "village pharmacy," and "panacea for all diseases." The seeds, leaves, flowers, and bark of the tree all have medicinal uses. The best part? It seems to work as a contraceptive both before and after sex. So, if you forget in the heat of the moment, you may not have to wait until the next day to get a morning-after pill that will make you feel like you have your period times a thousand. Animal studies have shown neem to be a potent contraceptive either taken internally (by males) or inserted into the vagina as a suppository or pessary. And the tests thus far have shown that fertility is regained soon after usage—there is no residual effect and it doesn't seem to affect hormones at all.

The seed and leaf extracts of the neem tree aren't just potentially spermicidal; they are also antimicrobial and antifungal and have antiviral properties. Yes, eco-sexuals—this wonder herb can potentially clear up yucky yeast and urinary tract infections and prevent the spread of herpes simplex virus type 2 and HIV.[28]

Neem oil is thought to kill sperm in the vagina within thirty seconds and be effective for up to five hours. Most traditional spermicide creams must be reapplied at least every hour, and we all know how irritating that can be if we're lucky enough to have more than just a brief romp in the hay.

Nonoxynol-9, the most common spermicide in use, is essentially a detergent. If used frequently or overused in one session, it can cause inflammation to your nether regions and damage the cells of the vagina and cervix. And lots of guys find that it stings, which should tell us something. So even as it kills off pathogens, it can cause raw skin and therefore make you more susceptible to HIV, herpes, and other not-so-fun diseases. Neem is far gentler, so let's hope it gets FDA approval soon.

# Birth Control Pills

We'll give the Pill its due: it did indeed change the world. Feminists give thanks to Simone de Beauvoir and Betty Friedan, but the Pill set us free in radical ways. Margaret Sanger, a lifelong advocate for women's rights and birth control, underwrote the research for the birth control pill in the 1950s and raised $150,000 for the project, which had a huge impact on women's lives in the second half of the twentieth century. Unfortunately, there was no way for us to foresee the environmental and health problems the pill would engender years later. The EPA has found that excreted or discarded birth control pills are ending up in our waterways, where they have a DNA-altering, gender-bending effect on fish and marine life. Any woman who's been on the Pill or considered it has heard that it can cause health complications after the age of thirty-five and for smokers, but it gets worse, far worse. Pharmaceutical literature warns of migraines, strokes, high blood pressure, blood clots, and heart attacks for women with certain risk factors. These may be rare side effects, but they should serve as a warning: a woman's cycle should not be trifled with. We ovulate, and then we menstruate in order to cleanse our bodies of eggs that haven't been fertilized. This natural process is inhibited by the Pill, which serves to trick the body into thinking that it is pregnant all the time. It shuts off ovulation. Many women, after years of being on the Pill, find that they can't get pregnant for months or years later—their fertility can be impaired over the long term. They are warned, in fact, not to try to get pregnant for some time after stopping the Pill because it depletes folate, a nutrient needed by pregnant women in order to prevent spina bifida in their babies. Studies have also found that oral contraceptives deplete several nutrients, including vitamins $B_2$, $B_6$, and $B_{12}$, zinc, vitamins C and E, magnesium, and even coenzyme Q10. These nutrient depletions have far-reaching effects; they can contribute to everything from depression, migraines, and anemia to cervical dysplasia—the precursor to cervical cancer.[29] They can also cause inflammation, even in young women. Many gynecologists are Pill happy—they prescribe the Pill for the bulk of sexually active women in monogamous relationships if they're under thirty-five and don't smoke. And that doesn't even include the dermatologists who prescribe it for their acne-prone patients. It's true that the higher-estrogen pills of the past were more dangerous, but the ones being prescribed today can still wreak full-on havoc with your body's precious ecosystem. And there is one last, rather scary item. Anecdotally, many women have revealed that their experience with the Pill made them question their sanity. Its effects on the hormones are such that being on it can make you feel like you have full-throttle PMS all the time, every day of the month. There are stories of women becoming violent with their partners, imagining affairs, and even feeling like they were being followed home by imaginary predators. Just Google "the Pill made me crazy," and go through some of the hundreds of postings on message boards.

With all of this in mind, consider that the Pill is probably also causing our fish to become transgendered. We ingest these pills and flush them back out into the oceans when we urinate. Hermaphroditic fish are a very bad development for the ecosystem, and the birth control pill should be an eco-sexual's very last choice.

## Diaphragms and Cervical Caps

Greenwise, diaphragms and cervical caps beat out condoms because they're not disposable, but they have higher failure rates than other methods. And when used alone, they're not for people who need to prevent STDs. They also require some form of spermicide. Many men and women are allergic to irritating conventional spermicides. If you're not a fan of Nonoxynol-9 (who is?) but want to try a diaphragm, there are alternatives. Women in the UK may know about the Honey Cap, a traditional diaphragm that's used with honey in place of conventional spermicide. Honey, which is antimicrobial and has been used for pregnancy prevention since antiquity, has had a well-deserved recent resurgence. All told, diaphragms and cervical caps aren't a bad choice on the eco-sexual scale of good, better, and best (at least for women in monogamous relationships).

## The Sponge

Elaine was right about a lot of things, but the sponge, although convenient, is not eco-friendly. It's made of nonrenewable plastic foam and spermicide. It can only be used once, and isn't biodegradable. Although the skin-to-skin contact may be nicer for those of us who hate condoms, the sponge just doesn't cut it.

## The Snip: Getting Your Tubes Tied

You've got to really know what you want from life to get to the snip stage, because the procedure to reverse it has been known to fail. Common candidates for this surgery are either male or female halves of long-term, monogamous couples. Bachelor guys who are absolutely sure they don't want kids have been known to go in for the big V on occasion, of course. For women, there's transabdominal sterilization, a type of tube tying that closes off a woman's fallopian tubes and prevents sperm from fertilizing her eggs. Depending on a woman's health and weight, different kinds of surgery are recommended, some that permit leaving the hospital the same day as the procedure and others that have a recovery period of a few days.

In a vasectomy, the vas deferens from each testicle is clamped, then tied or sealed, preventing swimmers from escaping. There is still ejaculation, but the sperm are kept out of the ejaculate and are reabsorbed back into the body. It can be done in an office or clinic and takes about thirty minutes, and recovery is quick. Note that men can still get their partners pregnant for a few months afterward, so use another method during that phase.

## The IUD

At this stage of our evolution as eco-sexuals, it turns out the IUD, or the intrauterine device, is our best option. Aside from the fact that it's 99 percent effective, the IUD lasts for ten years, and it's just a tiny bit of T-shaped plastic wrapped in copper (an inexpensive and readily available metal). It is inserted into the uterus at the doctor's office and removed when you want to get preggers. The IUD is still popular in Europe, but it got a very bad reputation in the United States in the 1970s after it was reported to cause pelvic infections and death. It turned out that these were false reports, but the damage to the IUD's public image has lasted. Women who prefer barrier-free sex should get over it and get one inserted (if they are in a monogamous relationship). If your sperm-filled partner doesn't want to go for the snip and you're not ready to tie up your own tubes, it's the best thing out there for your body and the environment.

# Getting a Bit More Risky with Your Frisky— Natural Methods of Contraception

Note: The alternative contraceptive methods in this section are not even close to foolproof. So if you are absolutely sure that you don't want to end up with child, use a barrier method while in early stages of experimentation, or be prepared for the consequences. In addition, consult with a local herbalist or naturopath who can work with you and observe the changes in your body and determine the best route.

## *Got Rhythm? Try Natural Fertility*

Even if you don't plan to have kids now or ever, a lot of infertile women out there would give an arm for your eggs and the symptoms that indicate that they're working. So don't curse your monthly curse— Aunt Flo and her cousin, ovulation, are your friends. They are a sign that your reproductive system is working the way it should. The bottom line is that every female eco-sexual should understand her cycles and feel blessed by them. Using this knowledge for contraception is another step entirely, one that should be considered carefully. For those in a monogamous relationship, the oh-so-natural rhythm method can be a lovely option. It allows for skin-to-skin contact, and there's nothing messy to apply before getting down to business. If you're not quite ready for kids or don't want any more, however, it's a bit of a risk, because it can definitely fail. You have to be willing to abstain from unprotected intercourse when you're ovulating, and you have to keep careful track of the various stages of your cycle throughout the month. If you don't trust yourself, don't want to bother with the tracking, or are unwilling to use a barrier method or practice sexual activities other than intercourse during that time, then fertility awareness probably isn't for you. And for single girls with one or more partners, the risk of STDs just isn't worth it. But, if you're committed to your partner and you know that he's faithful and STD free, fertility awareness is a great option. Finally, you've got to have a relatively stable menstrual cycle in order to be a candidate. So if your periods are usually erratic, use another method of birth control.

If you're a lucky lady with an average cycle and a faithful guy, get yourself a fertility calendar or just pop your info into the nifty online calculator at ovulation-calculator.org and see when you're likely to ovulate next. Keeping good records is the key to successfully mastering fertility awareness. Another option is to get yourself a red marker and put a giant *P* on your calendar, with the number of days in your cycle. Your cycle always begins on the first day of your period. So if you last bled twenty-seven days ago, you'll write "P 27." For most women, ovulation takes place fourteen days before menstruation, give or take two days. Eggs can only be fertilized within twenty-four hours of being released from the ovary. But because it's hard to isolate the exact moment of ovulation without a fertility kit, you will need to abstain during a five-day window. Since pesky, hearty sperm can remain viable up to three days in the body, this is a wise move. (Some even think those little swimmers can live for up to seven days, so who knows what kind of dice you're really rolling.)

## Signs of Ovulation

In addition to tracking the dates of your cycle, you should look for telltale signs of ovulation. Some women feel a twinge or two of ovulatory pain around this time—sometimes referred to as mittel-schmerz. Everyone is different, but many women notice telltale "egg white" mucus, the cervical fluid released at ovulation. It feels different than typical vaginal discharge and has a stretchy quality.

## Too Hot To Handle: Take Your Basal Body Temperature

Your body temperature can also help you figure out when you're about to ovulate. In order to track your temperature, you will need to download a free basal body temperature chart, available on just about any pregnancy website.

A basal body temperature chart provides a good visual basis for determining ovulation. Every morning, before getting out of bed or going to the bathroom, take your temperature. You can buy a special basal body temperature thermometer at the drugstore—most people recommend this over a standard thermometer. Start on day 1 of your cycle (the day you get your period) and write down your temperature. Repeat each day, and notice what your average daily temperature is. While your follicles are emitting estrogen, your body stays on the cool side. On the day of your ovulation, there will be a slight temperature shift. Just after ovulation, there should be a rise of approximately 0.4 to 0.6 degrees Fahrenheit (about 0.2 degrees Celsius). On the following two days your temperature will climb higher. After you've had a three-day period of consistently higher temps, you're most likely no longer fertile; let the fun begin. You will have to chart for a few cycles before you get the hang of this and know when ovulation is beginning.

## *Wild Carrot*

Herbalists have been successful, anecdotally, with wild carrot or Queen Anne's lace, an herb thought to have been used for contraception for at least two thousand years. Wild carrot grows abundantly in many areas of the world (but don't go picking it from your yard, because it is hard to distinguish from deadly water hemlock). It's probably better as a natural morning-after pill than as a reliable method of contraception across the cycle. So if you're using a barrier method and it fails, you can ostensibly take wild carrot seeds during ovulation to prevent implantation. Do be careful, though, because if it doesn't work and you do get pregnant, it can potentially harm a fetus. Wild carrot is also thought to be useful for mild bladder infections. Learn more at SisterZeus.com.

# Your Choice

No woman wants to have to terminate a pregnancy. But every year, when birth control methods inevitably fail, millions of women will make this choice. It is not easy, nor is it flip, as some anti-choice zealots would have you believe. Despite the decision of Roe v. Wade in the United States, access to abortion is still something that certain politicians and right-wing religious groups would like to take away from you (or your partner). With the climate around health care such as it is, this issue is not going away any time soon. There are forces working, as you read this, to strip you of access to affordable, safe, and legal abortion services from your doctor or the local clinic. (Not to mention those who stand outside of abortion clinics shouting at the doctors, nurses, and patients who walk through the doors.) Organizations like Planned Parenthood, NARAL, and NOW exist to protect your rights to your own body.

Women have been terminating unwanted pregnancies since antiquity, using herbs, acupuncture, and massage. In our world, these methods are considered "self-induced abortion" because they're practiced outside the medical system. These methods are controversial, especially given the already tense conversation around the topic of abortion. But with the help of a qualified herbalist or other holistic health professional, they can be viable alternatives for women who either lack access to medical abortion or prefer not to go that route.

For a more comprehensive look at these methods, read *Natural Liberty: Rediscovering Self-induced Abortion Methods* by the Sage-Femme Collective, which can be found at www.naturalliberty.org.

# Aunt Flo and the Eco-Sexual

When a woman's little friend is coming into town, she needs to steer clear of products that will wreck her system and the earth. If you want to go totally green during your time of the month, go for a menstrual cup. This totally reusable gizmo folds up and is placed high in the vagina, where it works, in a way, like a diaphragm. But its purpose is to collect your flow, which you then flush down the toilet or sink. The Keeper and the Diva Cup are two popular options. Made of medical-grade silicone, the Diva Cup is recommended to be replaced once a year. The Keeper is made from natural gum latex, and the company recently introduced a version made of silicone for people with latex allergies. If you were previously a tampon user and convert to cupping, you'll be flushing far less.

Jade and Pearl sustainably harvested natural sea sponges are reusable for up to six months. This is the kind of sponge I can get behind. (My apologies to Elaine.)

Even with all of these terrific eco-friendly options, sometimes you just want a tampon. But conventional tampons are made with bleached cotton, and the bleach can be harmful to the delicate skin inside your vagina and leach into your body quite easily. Instead, use tampons that are made from unbleached, natural cotton. Do try to go for the nonapplicator kind; these are greener than the cardboard applicator version. Maxim makes nonapplicator natural cotton tampons, and Natracare has been on the market for a long time and is a very reliable option as well.

Some women just feel better when they don't have to put anything inside, and a lot of chicks prefer not to have a tampon in overnight, in order to avoid risking toxic shock syndrome. Pads can be a necessary evil. Reusable cloth menstrual pads are economical and better for the earth than the disposable kind. Some companies are making them from hemp, organic cotton, and bamboo. GladRags are among the best-known reusable pads. But antihippie types may scoff at this kind of Earth Mother tribute, and some women simply don't want to deal with their own blood. So, although some conventional disposable menstrual pads are antiquated things that may remind you of *Are You There God? It's Me, Margaret*, there are a bunch of excellent natural alternatives on the market. Both Maxim and Natracare make pads in a variety of sizes and shapes.

# Sexually Transmitted Diseases

*Everything that used to be a sin is now a disease.*
—Bill Maher

To prevent all disease, including STDs, it's extremely important to keep the immune system in tip-top shape. The lower your immunity, the more susceptible you are to any virus or infection that tries to get into your system. Eating whole foods, drinking lots of water, avoiding alcohol and drugs, getting enough sleep, and increasing your intake of raw, green, leafy vegetables will help you to fight off most infections and viruses. You may not find garlic terribly sexy, but it contains the compound allicin, which is a powerful natural antibiotic.

# Human Papillomavirus (HPV)

HPV is the most common STD; at least 50 percent of the population will have a strain of it at some point in their lives. Interestingly, HPV mostly clears up on its own. The Pap test identifies cervical dyplasia caused by HPV, which can in certain cases lead to cervical cancer. Although this is rare, it is the reason that gynecologists are so vigilant about diagnosing Pap abnormalities. Conventional treatment is often painful and traumatic. The herb thuja has been used to treat HPV, but this should definitely be done with the guidance of a health care professional. Folic acid is sometimes prescribed as a preventative, and beta-carotene can help the body resist infection as well.

# Urinary Tract Infections

A lot of women get urinary tract infections after sex—not a disease per se, but it's painful and frustrating enough to be on this list. It also has the simplest solution of all: drink cranberry juice. This is an alternative method that really works—scientific studies back it up. Compounds in cranberry may prevent bacteria, such as E. coli, from clinging to cells along the walls of the urinary tract and causing infection. Moderate use of cranberry juice is a great preventative for those who are prone to urinary tract infections. If you don't get them regularly and want it to stay that way, probably the best preventative measure is to empty your bladder completely both right before and right after sex. If you do get one, you should get checked out by the doc so that it doesn't become more serious, because that wouldn't be fun for anyone, would it?

# Yeast Infections

Let she who has never had a yeast infection cast the first douche. Pesky *Candida albicans* is found in small amounts in healthy vaginas. It only becomes a problem when there is massive overgrowth. That's when the symptoms that will not be named begin. Pregnancy, menopause, diabetes, or taking antibiotics, birth control pills, or steroids are all factors that can encourage yeast overgrowth. Probiotic supplements, vinegar douches, topical tea tree oil cream or suppositories, and vaginal suppositories made with garlic or boric acid are often used to treat yeast infections. Regular consumption of *Lactobacillus acidophilus*, a type of beneficial bacteria normally found in the vagina, can help with prevention. A daily dose of real yogurt, not the horribly sugary kind, can keep the yeasties at bay. Make sure to find brands made from organic, hormone-free milk, with real active cultures.

# Pelvic Inflammatory Disease

Pelvic inflammatory disease (PID) is an extremely uncomfortable condition that can involve lower abdominal pain, fever, and discharge. It can also lead to infertility, so don't take it lightly. If home remedies like those mentioned below don't work, don't delay a trip to the gyno. If you're prone to PID, avoid iron supplements unless they're prescribed by your doctor. Iron helps bacteria "take root" in the cervix. Beta-carotene (preferably from foods like carrots, pumpkins, or acorn squash) helps the cells of the cervix resist reinfection by the bacteria associated with PID. It's also important to avoid vitamin C deficiency, whether by eating at least five servings of fruits and vegetables a day or by taking at least 160 mg of vitamin C a day. Vitamin C helps the lining of the cervix make the collagen "glue" that holds cells together and prevents infection. Also try taking long dan cao (Chinese gentian root) tea, which eliminates problem bacteria in the vagina while reducing pain and removing unpleasant vaginal discharge. Another treatment for PID is to apply plain, sugarless yogurt to your vulva and vagina, leaving it on for three hours then rinsing, once a day for three days. The common bacteria causing PID is *Gardnerella vaginalis*, and superhero *Lactobacillus* is poisonous to *Gardnerella vaginalis*.

## Chlamydia

The big C is another dangerous STD that should not be toyed with. Some general approaches for prevention and faster healing are available, but you need to take antibiotics if you have chlamydia. In addition, though, garlic acts as a natural antibiotic and aids healing, and kelp, a mineral, can be helpful. Vitamin B complex, vitamin C (a buffered form), vitamin E, and coenzyme Q10 are helpful supplements for healing. Some good herbs are astragalus, echinacea, goldenseal, pau d'arco, and red clover. If you're on antibiotics for this or any other infection, don't forget to take acidophilus, because it will help replenish friendly bacteria and prevent yeast infections.

## Herpes

Herpes is one of the STDs for which high immunity is extremely important. If you have the virus already, treat your body like a temple every day. You can reduce the amount of outbreaks you have this way, even though there is no true cure. Avoid caffeine like the plague. Foods high in the amino acid arginine have been found to trigger herpes outbreaks, so use caution if you're exploring the arginine-rich pro-sex diet mentioned in the previous chapter. Instead, search for foods high in lysine, an amino acid that helps control outbreaks. Yogurt, some cheeses, fruit (apricots, apples, pears), nuts, grains, and veggies are helpful. Try wheat germ, corn, winter squash, peas, pumpkin seeds, pistachios, peanuts, almonds, sesame seeds, and Brazil nuts. Neem has also been found to help with viral infections. The research is still preliminary, but it seems to have applications both as a topical treatment (soap, cream) and as internal medicine for herpes.

# Lubes

There's a lot more to your K-Y than meets the eye. Most conventional personal lubricants contain ingredients that your private parts do not want to be friends with. The ideal pH for a healthy vagina is between 2 and 3.2—vaginas are naturally acidic. Glycerin, a derivative of the soap-making process, strips the vagina of natural moisture and interferes with the body's ability to self-clean—thus causing yeast infections. Even scarier, it creates just the type of environment in which STD transmission is likely. So how's this for cruel irony? Glycerin is common in conventional personal lubricants. Many drugstore lubes also contain parabens or are derived from petroleum. You think you're doing yourself and your partner a favor when you lube up, but if you're using traditional lubes you're doing just the opposite. Here are some excellent alternatives (but note that none of the following have any contraceptive ingredients):

**Intimate Ecology**, a certified organic therapeutic personal lubricant and moisturizer with yogurt bioferment and probiotic peptides, is a totally unique product line—there has never been anything like it available commercially. It's the first product launch by Herbologie (herbologie.com), developed by Wisconsin-based phytochemist Elizabeth Moriarty, a woman who has an astonishing compendium of knowledge about your nether regions. Intimate Ecology is a line of therapeutic personal lubricant moisturizers specifically formulated to meet the intimate health care needs of women. It incorporates therapeutic botanicals, a pH adjuster, lactobacillus extracts—or "skin yogurt"—and probiotic peptides. More than simply providing moisture, it makes you healthier than you were before you used it. Hell, you should use it even if you're celibate.

**Yes Yes Yes** (yesyesyes.org) is a UK-based line of stylishly packaged organic personal lubricants. They are free of parabens, glycerin, hormones, silicones, and petroleum products, and—even better—they're certified organic.

**Firefly Organics** (organiclubricant.com) makes a personal lubricant that isn't compatible with latex condoms but will work with polyurethane. Their formulation is shea-butter based and free of glycerin, parabens, and petroleum products.

**Sliquid** (sliquid.com) makes lubes that are glycerin and paraben free and offers both a water-based and a silicone-based formula. They're vegan, latex safe, and condom-friendly.

Health is eco-wealth, and there's nothing sexier. Now you've got to find another eco-sexual with whom to share your bounty. Onward and greenward.

# PART III

# MORE ECO-SEXY OPTIONS FOR THE ECOLOGICAL ADVENTURER

# CHAPTER EIGHT

# LOOKING FOR MR. (OR MS.) GOODPLANET: HOW TO FIND AND KEEP CARBON-NEUTRAL LOVE

You can waste a whole lot of time and money trying to find your eco-soul mate on traditional dating sites like eHarmony.com. Luckily, lonely eco-sexuals who want to network with their own kind have tons of options, and more come online all the time. No matter how attuned your "greendar" is, with these sites, you'll know exactly what you're getting.

## Connecting with Your Eco-Sexual Tribe

Whatever your pleasure, there's a dating site to fit your taste. Environmentalists, vegetarians, vegans, raw-foodists, ethical warriors, volunteers, and even plain vanilla Democrats have their niches on the Web. The caveat here is that not all of these sites may have members in your area, so you have to "pays your money and takes your chances." Or actually, sign up for a profile and take your chances, since most of the sites below are fee free.

concernedsingles.com

earthwisesingles.com

ecodater.com

ecohookups.com

ethicalsingles.com

ethicalvegandating.com

evolver.net

greendrinks.org*

greenfriends.com

green-passions.com

greenspeeddating.com

natural-friends.com

rawfoodfriends.com

spiritualsingles.com

vegetarianpassions.com

wholeearthfriends.com

* Greendrinks.org is not a dating site; it's a hub for a self-organizing global network of greenies that meet in local bars in hundreds of cities all over the world once a month. But eco-sexual hotties attend their events, so do check them out.

If you don't have any luck with the sites listed above and must stick to conventional dating sites, be an eco-detective and use search keywords that will appeal to the ones you want to woo. In addition to obvious keywords like *eco-friendly*, *green*, and *environmentalist*, search for *conscious*, *progressive*, *garden*, *animals*, *sustainable*, *locavore*, *yoga*, or whichever green buzzwords really get you buzzed.

# Getting Numbers for Your Little Green Book

If you're a total Luddite and don't want to surf for your eco-sexual catch online, socialize at venues where Mr. or Ms. Right is most likely to hang out. Use meetup.com to find eco-events in your area

# Going Where the Greenies Are:
# The Greenest Cities Around the Globe

If you're living what feels like a lame little life in a lame little town and you're ready for a change, check out the fifteen greenest cities in the world (according to Grist.org in 2008[30]). You might just find green love if you broaden your horizons. Or at least consider taking a vacation to one of these green venues. One of the major things that many of the following locations have in common is walkability and excellent public transportation.

1. **Reykjavik, Iceland.** Hello Bjork! This city boasts hydrogen buses and geothermal and hydropower energy sources.

2. **Portland, Oregon, United States.** With tons of beautiful places to play outdoors, this city is often at the top of green city lists. In addition, it has light rail, buses, bike lanes, and seventy-four miles of trails—not to mention a citywide passion for local and organic foods, high recycling rates, a huge biking culture, and more.

3. **Curitiba, Brazil.** There are probably tons of hotties here, and because the city offers 580 square feet of green space per person, they're having a lot of fun outdoors. They also have a flock of thirty lawn-trimming sheep and almost everyone takes public transport.

4. **Malmö, Sweden.** Several neighborhoods in this city aim to make it an *ekostaden* ("eco-city") along social, environmental, and economic lines. Also, there are extensive parks and green space here. Extra points if you're a brunette—you'll get a date before you unpack your suitcase.

5. **Vancouver, British Columbia, Canada.** Vancouver gets 90 percent of its power from renewable sources. They have two hundred parks and eighteen miles of waterfront, plus they have an actual one-hundred-year plan for sustainability.

6. **Copenhagen, Denmark.** Three words: *offshore wind farm*. Their new metro system, born in 2000, is a model of efficiency. Most people ride their bike to work.

7. **London, England.** London is on the way to switching over 25 percent of its power to locally generated sources, and cut its $CO_2$ emissions by 60 percent in twenty years.

8. **San Francisco, California, United States.** You may find your heart here after all. Half of the inhabitants of San Francisco take public transit, walk, or ride their bikes each day. Green space and parks cover 17 percent of the city. They've also banned nonrecyclable plastic bags.

9. **Bahía de Caráquez, Ecuador.** A haven for eco-tourists, this city has developed biodiversity programs and worked on controlling erosion after a devastating storm in the 1990s. They also compost organic waste from public markets and support organic agriculture and aquaculture.

10. **Sydney, Australia.** Searching for eco-sexuals here will give new meaning to the term "Down Under." Sydney, because of emissions trading, green power, and transport, considers itself carbon neutral.

11. **Barcelona, Spain.** From solar energy to pedestrian friendliness, this beautiful city is the perfect setting for your own green version of *Vicky Cristina Barcelona*.

*continued*

continued from previous page

12. **Bogotá, Colombia.** With a highly efficient bus system, pedestrian-friendly sidewalks, 180 miles of bike trails, and an annual car-free day, this city will allow you to breathe deeply as you court your eco-honey.

13. **Bangkok, Thailand.** They've really addressed the air pollution issues here and have a five-year green strategy. This includes recycling used cooking oil as biodiesel and curbing emissions.

14. **Kampala, Uganda.** They support urban agriculture here, and they are removing urban taxis in favor of an efficient bus system.

15. **Austin, Texas, United States.** By 2020, Austin will cover 20 percent of its electricity bills with renewable energy. It has 30 miles of bike trails, and 15 percent of its land is devoted to green space. If you add in the great music and yearly festivals, you will have found yourself one great place to live as an open eco-sexual.

and attend them just like you would hit the local bar. Frequent your neighborhood locavore restaurant and don't be shy about sitting alone at the bar with a glass of biodynamic Pinot. Spend extra time in the café at your local health food store, lingering over a book. Go to flea markets and vintage stores. Try parks, beaches, hiking trails— all the places you would take your beloved if he or she were only in your life already.

# Reach Out and Touch Someone

Part and parcel of being in a budding relationship, or even a casual flirtation, is communication. Whether you meet online or in person, you'll be exchanging digits, calling and texting each other, and instant-messaging sweet nothings as part of courtship. So greening your tech life is integral to greening your sex life. Working Assets is a socially responsible mobile phone company. But there isn't really an eco-friendly cell phone—any claims about these are mostly hype. Samsung's Reclaim cell phone moves in the right direction, with 40 percent of its outer casing made of a bioplastic made from corn, and a charger that lets you know when it's finished charging so you can unplug it. But within your phone's circuit board you can find antimony, arsenic, beryllium, cadmium, coltan, copper, lead, mercury, and nickel. When it's time to invest in a cell phone, remember to dispose of your old one responsibly. Thoroughly research electronics recycling companies, because some of them are in bed with the recycling industry's version of the black market and the toxins in your phone could end up in the wrong place. And if you want to keep yourself safe from the ravages of cell phone radiation, try a Safe Space phone patch (safespaceprotection.com). These nifty little stickies are thought to neutralize electromagnetic radiation.

## Alternative Energy: Going Solio

If you're dating someone you like, you'd better not get caught without juice to power your gadgets. You never know—a delayed email response, a missed text message, or a mislaid voicemail just might lower your chances of scoring. (Those who call late on Saturday afternoon for Saturday night dates, take note and ask in advance.) You can avoid that kind of mess by keeping a Solio (solio.com) on hand. This amazing universal hybrid charger is solar powered (although it can also take a charge from a standard electrical outlet). An hour of sunshine equals twenty minutes of talk time. It's a great emergency power source that will keep you from getting caught with your pants down. (Save that part for later.)

# The Date

An eco-hottie is willing to go out with you—you'd best make it count.

## Getting There

The first thing to think about while planning an eco-date is transportation. Since the beginning of time, it seems, the traditional date has followed a particular pattern. There's the 1950s version: Boy meets girl, boy calls girl, boy asks girl out on date, and boy picks up girl in car for said date. That's all changed, and you can be a part of the new way of doing things, even if you don't live in one of the eco-friendly cities listed earlier in the chapter. Some suitors will drive around in preparation for a date (to pick up flowers, for instance), then drive to a date's house, then drive to the destination, then drive the date home, and then drive him- or herself home (sometimes that night and sometimes the next morning). Must we be so antiquated? Of course, you get eco-points if you drive a hybrid or electric car, but most of us aren't there yet. Eco-sexuals need to totally rethink car culture. Chivalry is nice, but your date can meet you halfway, especially if it's easier for one of you to take public transportation. If you live in the suburbs or exurbs, where walking to your date is impossible, you've got to get creative. A biking date is a terrific option.

# First Date: Getting Adventurous—Extracurricular Eco-Sexual Activities

You're not a freaky nudist (not that there's anything wrong with that). You're just a freestylin' single on the make for a fellow greenie, or you're an environmentalist in the throes of a new relationship, or perhaps you're dating three people at once. Wherever you find yourself on this spectrum, you want to spice things up before the two of you fall into bed. The most obvious, natural choice of activities for eco-friendly first (or second or third) dates is anything in the great outdoors. Go hiking, biking, to the beach (even in winter), or a local park, or just for a nice long walk. Don't get caught up in the idea that you must spend money on a date; you're not that old-fashioned, are you? Besides, you'll get to know your soon-to-be lover a lot better strolling through a beautiful, natural scene than you would in a loud bar or at an intimate dinner when you're nervous as hell and on your best behavior. A simple walk gets your blood moving, takes the pressure off, and creates instant subject matter about which you can chat. If you really want to impress another eco-sexual, set up a volunteering date. Pitch in to clean up a blighted community, help paint a school with low-VOC paints, or plant a community garden.

# Second Date: Into Your Lair (or His or Hers)

All that hard work has paid off, almost. Once you've snagged yourself a second date with a like-minded potential soul mate, it's time to show off what you know. What do eco-sexuals do on dates? Mostly the same stuff that regular people do on dates, like having dinner. Nothing shows off your eco-knowledge like cooking an organic meal for your soon-to-be lover (for recipes, see chapter 4). Amanda Young, holistic health and nutrition coach, Sensual Eating workshop leader, and founder of Urban Goddess Health, has been kind enough to share her tips for sensual eating. (She's also a chocolatier. For more delicious tips, visit urbangoddesschocolate.com.)

**Who:** Sensual eating can be done alone or in a group, but it probably brings the most pleasure when shared with one special someone.

**Where:** Create an ambiance that draws you out of your mind and into your senses. Candles, cushions on the floor, and aromatherapy oils all start to slowly invite you into the moment.

**What:** Choose foods with interesting textures. Start with something very simple like a strawberry and work your way up to creamy chocolate truffles or salty, sustainably harvested caviar that explodes in your mouth. Make it a four-course extravaganza! And remember to use only organic foods (they really do taste much better).

Now that the scene is set, bring out that precocious "in the moment" energy of your sensuous inner child. With each of the following steps, take your t-i-m-e. Linger in the moment.

**See:** Take in the visual. Imagine that you have never seen this food before. Notice subtle variations in color, shape, and texture.

**Touch:** Feel the texture of the food. Experience the sensation without naming it. Allow yourself to play with the concept of touch. How would it feel to rub that cool strawberry on your face?

**Smell:** Bring the food up to your nose and, without naming it, experience the aroma. You may notice that your mouth starts to water. Your senses are responding to the anticipation of the coming satisfaction.

**Bite:** As you bring the food close to your mouth, pay attention to how your lips part automatically and your tongue prepares to accept the morsel. And please, allow that tongue to be free. We don't allow our tongues to roam freely nearly enough in our eating experiences. When the tongue is ready, it will maneuver the food between your teeth, and then the moment has arrived. Allow your teeth to bite down and release the explosion of flavors in your mouth.

**Taste:** This is where the edible fireworks reach their height. Your taste receptors are all lit up. Is the flavor sweet, sour, juicy? Stay with the sensation. How much pleasure can one bite of a berry bring?

**Swallow:** Continue chewing and tasting slowly, and you will notice that the taste and consistency begin to change. When they are no longer bringing pleasure and you are ready to swallow the food, do so with absolute consciousness. Allow yourself to be still and feel the experience of being one bite fuller as the food reaches your belly. Take a deep breath in and notice if you feel increased awareness and sensitivity in any other areas of your body.

## Third Date and Beyond: Tantric Sex—Be Here Now

It's really progressing, isn't it? You're ready to really impress your new "friend" without harming the environment in the process. *Tantra* is a Sanskrit word that means "loom," "weaving," or "the carrying out of a ceremony," depending on one's interpretation. According to Barbara Carrellas, author of *Urban Tantra: Sacred Sex for the Twenty-first Century*, tantra was a spiritual rebellion that was the sex, drugs, and rock 'n' roll of its time. The ancients (in India, at least) believed that they needed to give up bodily pleasure in order to avoid endless reincarnation. Tantra was a sociopolitical movement that subscribed to the belief that enlightenment could be achieved in just one lifetime. Tantra is all about intentionality, directing energy, breath work, and eye gazing. But don't think only New Age types practice tantra. It's quite eco-sexual. Tantra doesn't use a single bit of the earth's resources, it provides hours and hours of fun, and it raises consciousness to a whole new level.

## Every Breath You Take

You don't have to read the entire *Kama Sutra* or spend hours holding off on orgasm in order to experiment with tantra. Start with remembering how to breathe. Even as you sit and read these words, bring your attention to your breath and think about whether it's flowing deeply, fast, slow, or barely at all. A quick tantra trick is to try to synchronize your breathing to your partner's or, in some cases, the one you'd like to be your partner. Say you're on a date and you're not connecting because the person sitting across from you is nervous and fidgeting. Sometimes all it takes to calm a person down is to tune in to his or her breath and match it. Even if you can't hear the person breathing over the clanking of dishes in a restaurant, try to get a sense of it by watching his or her chest move up and down. This can also work when you're in bed with someone and things aren't going well, by the way.

## More than Meets the Nondominant Eye

"In tantra, sex is not an action. It is not one more thing that humans *do*. Sex is an energy that exists on its own," explains Barbara Carrellas. Practitioners of tantra believe that gazing into the nondominant eye (the left if the person is right-handed, and vice versa) is a means of gazing into the soul. This can invite a somewhat frightening level of intimacy with a partner, so it's not for the faint of heart. Carrellas suggests that you practice it by yourself, with a mirror, in order to grow brave enough to do it with a partner. She believes that you can achieve the "great cosmic orgasm" with enough practice.

### Tantric Games

Here is a basic tantra exercise, one that even those who have practiced for years continue to go back to. Sit face-to-face with your partner. Maintain a gentle gaze with your left eye into your partner's nondominant eye for several minutes. Next, bring your awareness to the rise and fall of his or her belly and chest as your partner breathes in and out. Place your hand on his or her stomach and feel the expansion and contraction there. Notice whether you've synchronized your breathing. Listen to the breaths and add a sound with your exhale. Continue for at least ten minutes. This is some serious stuff, and it can feel more intimate than sex.

### Going Deeper

This one is lots of fun and takes some restraint. Let's say you've already become very aroused with heavy petting or whatever turns you on. Stop. Separate slightly, so your bodies are no longer touching. Then go back to synchronizing your breathing and gazing into each other's nondominant eye. Then visualize moving the sexual energy you're feeling from your belly throughout your whole body. Then direct it to your partner. It's amazing what you can accomplish without doing the actual deed.

# Other Games Eco-Sexuals Play

This is, after all, a book about sex. So if you're done with psychospiritual enlightenment and are ready to get down to business, the next chapter will give a whole new meaning to the phrase "playing with toys."

# ECO-BABES in TOYLAND: green PLAYTHings for THE BeDROOM

Pull that well-worn sex toy out of your nightstand drawer and take a good, hard look at it. Perhaps it's brought you much pleasure, but did you ever stop to think about what it's actually made of? Considering where the thing goes, you really should take stock of the materials that give your little friend his always-friendly shape and size. Old-school vibrators are full of dangerous substances. *Off-gassing* is a problem under ordinary circumstances, but imagine how much worse these chemicals can be in the warm, moist environment

**OFF-GASSING:** "New car smell" is the most familiar association we have with off-gassing. Products fresh from the factory continue to release toxins from the manufacturing process even as they sit on shelves and enter your home. This can make anyone sick, but the toxins are particularly dangerous to those with compromised immune systems and allergies.

between our legs. It's safe to say that if you bought your vibe before 2000, it's not safe. But if you're unsure, you can always do the smell test. Give it a good sniff—does it smell like a vinyl shower curtain? If so, you can bet your bottom dollar that it's full of stuff you don't want in your nether regions.

According to the Coalition for Toxic Toys (CATT; badvibes.org), if your toy has lost its sheen, is cracked, or has changed shape since you purchased it, it's time to say buh-bye. It's always better not to throw old possessions into the landfill, of course. Luckily, if you're parting with your old buddy, you will appreciate the new sex toy recycling program. The Green Business Partnership, a division of Dreamscapes, will take care of the dirty business. Just ship your old items to Dreamscapes Recycling Program, 5450 Bruce B Downs Boulevard #366, Wesley Chapel, FL 33544. (Check recycleyoursextoy.com for more information.)

## Don't Toy with Phthalates

Back in the day before alternatives existed, sex shop purveyors with integrity often told their customers to carefully wash their toys and to put condoms on them before use. Why? Because the vast majority of toys were porous and leaked chemical goo, and the experts knew it. The "Made in China" label on most novelty sex toys said it all. And most sex toys are indeed marked "novelty" because of antiquated laws that govern their usage. The use of sex toy ingredients, and their effects on human health, however, are largely unregulated. Because, you know, you're using it as a *novelty*—not as a sex toy.

In order to make a hard plastic soft, you need to "plasticize" it. And the cheapest go-to ingredient has been phthalates up until the last few years. If your toy has been with you through thick and thin, between relationships and during them, it's old enough to toss (or rather, recycle), since it most likely contains phthalates. These chemical nasties are suspected of having carcinogenic and mutagenic affects on the skin and mucous membranes. Happily, they are being phased out in the United States and the European Union because consciousness is finally expanding and laws are changing. But the rule of thumb is that if you don't want it in the bottle that holds your water, you certainly don't want it in your dildo.

According to the Ethan Imboden, founder and chief creative of Jimmyjane (a manufacturer of sleek, beautifully designed, and eco-friendly sex toys), polyvinyl chloride and jelly materials are most often associated with phthalates, but they don't all contain it. And by the same token, silicone, the preferred material for eco-sex enthusiasts, sometimes does. So always check labels and shop trusted sources (see page 167). It's worth it to be vigilant here.

Let's also note that the Rabbit Habit vibrator, made famous by *Sex and the City* circa 2004, was once made strictly of phthalate-laden plastic. Now the manufacturer makes a safer version using elastomer.

# Playing It Safe

The brilliant and wise team behind Smitten Kitten, an awesomely progressive sex store in Minneapolis, has initiated a campaign to enlighten the public about the dangers of sex toys and healthier alternatives. Here is their "Smart Shoppers Tool Kit" (courtesy of CATT):[31]

Use the following tools and tips to make smart, informed decisions despite ill-informed store clerks, unreliable product packaging, and overwhelming options. These tips are meant as guides to help you make your own decisions!

1. **Implement the smell test.** Your sense of smell is your most reliable tool for identifying a potentially dangerous sex toy. If you smell any chemical odors or perfumes, you can assume that these odors are a direct result of a process known as off-gassing, in which myriad, unknown chemical compounds are migrating out of the material (usually PVC or polystyrene) and contaminating the air you breathe. There is concern that these "mystery" chemicals will also migrate onto your skin and into your body during the course of use. Safe 100 percent medical grade silicone toys do not smell because there are *no* chemicals present to off-gas.

2. **Be wary of claims that condoms will protect you from toxic toys.** If your salesperson or product literature suggests that you always use a condom over your sex toy, beware that this toy is potentially toxic. Safe sex toys made from 100 percent medical-grade silicone, high-quality glass, surgical steel, polished stone, or hard plastics including acrylic do not require the use of a condom because they can be thoroughly sanitized to prevent the exchange of microscopic organisms, including bacteria, fungi, and viruses that might cause infection. Remember that to prevent the transmission of infection, you must sanitize your toy before sharing it.

3. **Never take claims made on sex toy packaging at face value.** There is absolutely no requirement that the product packaging for sex toys or the literature contained therein be truthful in any way. Just because particular packaging might say a toy is made of silicone

does not mean it actually is! Sex toy manufacturers have gotten savvy (you might say tricky). They try to lure consumers to purchase products by falsely labeling them as safe. These toys are clearly labeled as silicone but contain only trace amounts of silicone and are instead riddled with much less savory ingredients!

Also, consider quality claims like "hygienically superior" to be baseless until convinced otherwise by your own good research or common sense. Be on the lookout for confusingly similar spellings of materials that you know are safe. For instance, never confuse silicon with silicone. The long and short story is, don't trust the packaging without supporting evidence.

Having said that, keep in mind that all reputable silicone toy manufacturers do clearly label their products as such. While this is certainly not an exhaustive list, some responsible and safe silicone toy makers include Tantus Silicone, Vixen Creations, Jollies, and Fun Factory.

4. **Be suspicious of space-age, overtly sexual or technical-sounding terms for sex toy materials.** One way to spot these faux "materials" is to look for the registered trademark symbol (®) following the "material" in question. If the term in question is trademarked, this means that it is a trade name and has been registered with the U.S. Patent and Trademark Office. If you see the (TM) symbol, this may mean that the user claims some exclusive rights to

use of the mark or word. Remember, no actual names of materials will ever be properly trademarked.

Know that these trademarked terms do not necessarily connote any specific chemical composition. They are instead marketing terms used by companies to differentiate and sell a particular product without making any specific claims or mention of the actual materials used in the production of the item in question.

This means that all of those directions about caring for "cyber\_\_\_\_\_" or "real\_\_\_\_\_" are suspect at best because these words are nothing more than a product marketing executive's smooth attempt to seduce you into buying the product because it sounds sexier or more technical than the competitor's.

For example, there is no reliable way to know what a toy that is labeled "cyber\_\_\_\_\_" is actually made of without full disclosure from the manufacturer or an independent chemical analysis by a qualified laboratory. Always wonder why a toy is labeled with a fancy name without also disclosing the ingredients!

To determine if a toy is safe, you must first determine the actual composition of the toy. Toys made from nontoxic and nonporous materials such as 100 percent medical-grade silicone, polished stone, surgical steel, high-quality solid glass, and hard plastics including acrylic are safe. You will notice that ® or TM symbols are not present following actual ingredients (as opposed to those made-up marketing terms) because you cannot claim intellectual property rights on such words.

Now that you know what to avoid, what do you really want in a new sex toy? See the sidebar below for tips.

One last word on vibes and other electric toys: look for ones with rechargeable batteries, like Jimmyjane's life-changing waterproof Form 6 (jimmyjane.com), or the discreet we-vibe (we-vibe.com). You might even like the hand-cranked Earth Angel (theearthangel.ie), with its own patented power core.

## Top Tips for Someone Shopping for Their First Sex Toy

*From Ethan Imboden of Jimmyjane*

**Start simple.** If vibration is a new sensation for you, you'll likely find that there's quite a bit of adventure available in that area alone. Consider simple, understandable products focused on clitoral stimulation, such as a bullet, smoothie, or external vibrator.

**Start approachable.** Trying a vibrator for the first time (particularly with another person present) is an exciting but potentially daunting prospect. You should consider designs that are unintimidating—smaller sizes, cleaner design, and good packaging and presentation can all help.

**Start beautiful.** Whether you are introducing a vibrator into partner sex or are intending to use it on your own, choosing a product that is aesthetically pleasing can help make this go smoothly. If anything should be beautiful, it's the objects involved in our sexuality.

# Notable Online and Brick-and-Mortar Sex Stores

These shops all carry safe and healthy sex toys, and most are owned by women. Do your best to buy your toys locally. This is just a small sampling; there are more and more nonsketchy, friendly, and fun sex shops opening all the time.

**Toys in Babeland** (babeland.com), based in Seattle, Washington, and New York City, was founded in 1993 by Claire Cavanah and Rachel Venning. It was one of the first hip, urban sex shops to cater to women. They were also pioneers with green sex toys, stocking safe

## Safe Sex Toy Retailers and Manufacturers

coco-de-mer.com

conezone.info

divine-interventions.com

eartherotics.com (their tagline is "doing it green")

funfactory.de

happyvalleysilicone.com

jildos.com

jimmyjane.com

lelo.com

liberator.com

luxotiq.com

miuzu.com

nexusrange.com

njoytoys.com

nobessence.com

pyrexions.com

tantusinc.com

we-vibe.com

alternatives before the rest of the industry got the memo on phthalates. The online store sells an "Eco-Sexy Kit" in an effort to promote green sex.

**Smitten Kitten** (smittenkittenonline.com), based in Minneapolis, Minnesota, carries a bevy of healthy toys (including handcrafted options). Jennifer Pritchett is the owner of this extremely cool and progressive store, and also the force behind the Coalition for Toxic Toys.

**Eve's Garden** (evesgarden.com), based in a discreet location in New York City, was the first women-owned-and-operated sex shop. Their mission statement is, in part, "to empower women to celebrate their sexuality as a positive, nourishing, and creative force in their lives."

**Coco De Mer** (coco-de-mer.com) specializes in "erotic luxury." Founded by Sam Roddick, the daughter of activist Anita Roddick (owner of The Body Shop), this delightful sex shop is full of ethical, green goodies. Coco De Mer just opened its first store in the States (in New York City). They sell rare erotic books and other exotic playthings, and they also host educational salons.

# Creative Juices:
# Eco-Friendly Massage Oils

Whether you're playing solo or with a partner, massage always enhances the mood. Massage has so many healthy fringe benefits aside from its pure pleasure principle that you'd be a fool to skip it. Massage relieves pain and tension, improves circulation, reduces stress, puts you (and your partner) in a better mood, rejuvenates you, and releases endorphins. Here are two incredibly simple recipes for massage oil.

## A Massage Oil for All Skin Types and Occasions

*For this massage oil, make sure you use an organic vegetable oil, like grape seed or jojoba oil.*

$1/2$ cup vegetable oil
$1/2$ cup almond oil
3 drops lavender essential oil

Mix all of the ingredients in a ceramic bowl. You may gently heat this oil, if you like. Try a low-impact heat source, such as holding the bowl above a candle flame for a short time.

Yield: 1 cup

## A Massage Oil for Lovers with Dry Skin

*For a warm massage, you can heat the oil a bit before adding it to the mixture. Just make sure it's not too hot before slathering it on!*

Handful of organic rose petals
$1/2$ cup warm water
$1/2$ cup olive oil, plus a few drops
$1/4$ cup organic shea butter

Grab a handful of organic rose petals and put them in a large bowl. Add the water (just enough to cover the petals). Then add a few drops of olive oil. Cover the bowl tightly and leave it overnight so the petals infuse the water. When you're ready for the massage, remove the petals and mix in the olive oil and shea butter.

## Ready-to-Use Massage Oils

No time to make your own? The following massage oils are sexy, silky, and very eco-friendly.

**Intimate Organics** (intimateorganics.com) has an extremely sexy variety of massage oils made from organic ingredients.

**Earthly Body** (earthlybody.com) oils are made from hemp seed oil; they are residue free and have a professional glide.

**Weleda** (weleda.com) has a great massage oil made from arnica that is incredibly restorative.

**Pangea Organics** (pangeaorganics.com) makes Pyrenees Lavender with Cardamom, which is hot and silky at once.

Now that you're good and dirty, it's time to think about sleeping and showering (so you can wake up and do it again tomorrow).

# CHAPTER TEN

# BED, BATH, AND WAY BEYOND: ECO-SEXING YOUR BOUDOIR

You're officially green in both body and soul, but what about your main domain? Just like it matters what you eat, which lotions and creams you rub into your skin, and what objects you insert, your surroundings have major impact as well. From the paint on your bedroom walls to the toxins in your shower curtain, your sleeping and bathing quarters—where you do most of your sexing and sex prep— are laden with hazards. Don't invite any potential paramours into your boudoir until you make it green.

## The Bedroom: Green Between the Sheets

Your bedroom is where the magic ostensibly happens, so don't neglect the details. Aside from the fact that we spend much of our lives supine and sleeping, there are a great many reasons to green your boudoir. First of all, making small eco-friendly changes can improve your health, and as we learned in a chapter 6, your health has everything to do with your libido. The tips in this chapter will make your bedroom into an incredibly sexy, healthy lair. So let's get started with the foundation of your sex life: your mattress.

## Sleeping with the Enemy

We spend approximately three thousand hours a year—one-third of our lives—in bed. Unfortunately, the traditional mattress industry gets away with scandalous behaviors; they have, until now, had a monopoly on our precious sleep. Let's leave aside the fact that they mark up their prices 100 to 200 percent and focus instead on the horror show that is the average store-bought mattress. The surface upon which we rest our weary heads and have our playful romps is one gigantic ecological disaster zone. Synthetic materials emitting poisonous chemicals are off-gassing right into your lungs as you try to dream of more pleasant things. Polyurethane foam, the substance most mattresses have been made of since the late 1960s, is a petroleum-based material that emits volatile organic compounds (better known as VOCs and also found in paint). Skin and lung irritation are but two possible side effects of polyurethane. Then there's formaldehyde. Yes, that awful-smelling liquid that you first encountered in a jar, containing a to-be-dissected frog in biology class. That formaldehyde, which serves as an adhesive in your mattress, is linked to allergies, asthma, and lung, nose, and throat cancers.

Flame-retardant chemicals are ubiquitous in conventional mattresses, and this situation has worsened because of the fear of going up in flames in the event of a fire (for example, falling asleep in bed with lit cigarettes in our hands). Before 2004, pentaBDE, a chemical dangerous to the liver, thyroid, and nervous system, was the toxic flame-retardant cocktail of choice, but it was phased out. Then, in 2007, a law was passed requiring all beds manufactured in or imported into the United States to pass an open-flame test. So now mattresses must be doused in a chemical bath of toxic substances, including antimony and boric acid, which have been known to leach into our skin. Unfortunately, if you've bought a bed since that time, you can't even find out what's in it, because the major mattress manufacturers have "proprietary blends" of flame retardant. They consider them trade secrets. An average queen innerspring mattress is thought to have about one and a half pounds of chemicals in the ticking. (This is a huge problem in crib mattresses, which will be important for you to know about if you forgot to read the birth control chapter.) Even memory foam, that NASA-inspired and Swedish-cultivated wonder material, is made from polyurethane. Then there are dust mites, a common problem in conventional mattresses. These creepy crawlies may be invisible to the naked eye, but they cause all manner of allergies.

It sounds horrible, but don't start sleeping on the floor just yet. There are many clean, green mattress options out there. The solutions developed by the alternative, organic, healthy mattress manufacturers of the world are simple: wool and latex. Wool is naturally inflammable, although it is not vegan. Look for wool made from certified cruelty-free farms with happy sheep. Natural latex is sustainable and free of those nasty chemicals mentioned above. Here's the lowdown if you're ready to throw down some cash for a new, organic mattress. Note that they are still pretty expensive, but they typically outlast conventional mattresses, and if you read the two preceding paragraphs, you know they're well worth the cost in health and wellness.

## Why Natural Latex Will Help You Have More Fun in Bed

The sweet and sustainable rubber tree grows on hilly slopes only within about 10 degrees of the equator. Latex mattresses are incredibly dense and have the support and give of a memory foam mattress, sans the chemicals. You'll be able to find mattresses that are about 95 percent natural latex, and that's more than good enough. Be careful when you shop, however, because synthetic latex products are coming on the market in larger numbers, as latex seems to be the next big thing in bedding. Even some of the conventional mattress manufacturers are jumping on this bandwagon, so make sure not to get greenwashed; choose only natural latex. Savvy Rest (savvyrest.com) is the go-to company for aweseome, comfortable, tailored-to-your-own-needs latex beds.

## Dunlop vs. Talalay: The Smackdown

Dunlop and Talalay are different processes by which natural latex is made. The kind and wonderful people behind the green mattress maker Savvy Rest have an information-rich website, including a page dedicated to the differences between these two methods. The original method, called the Dunlop, has been in use since 1929. The liquid latex is whipped with air to make a foam, poured into a mold, and heated until it vulcanizes. The process makes Dunlop mattresses slightly firmer on the bottom side. The Talalay method is more complex and higher tech, involving pouring, sealing, flash freezing, and stabilizing. It is more expensive because of the extra steps and has a more consistent cell structure.

## To Bounce or Not to Bounce, That Is the Question

Sex on a foam mattress has its benefits, even though some detractors say that losing the bounce means losing the fun. The truth is that when you move from an innerspring mattress to a foam one, whether it's natural latex or the yucky conventional kind, your sex probably won't be as athletic as it was before. Eco-sexuals report that sex on a foam mattress is a more intimate affair. You won't have the response of your partner's bod bouncing back at you, but you will have more stability to position yourself however you fancy. That means you can be more experimental. And when you eventually get to the sleeping part of sleeping with someone, your twists and turns won't bother your bedmate. If you're the vivacious type who can't live without a bit of bounce-back, check out some of the green innerspring options, like the Green Nest organic tufted innerspring mattress. This is made with traditional Bonnell-style coils and quilted layers of organic cotton and wool.

## Baby's Got Back Pain

If you're one of the millions who suffer from back pain, don't worry that eco-beds won't meet your needs. Many of the green bed manufacturers put just as much thought into ergonomics as they do sustainability. Savvy Rest's website offers an extensive frequently asked questions section and even a questionnaire on their website to make sure you get exactly the right mattress. This company gets seriously granular in order to make sure you get the best ergonomic and eco-friendly sleep possible.

## Other Green Mattress Options

If you're not a fan of latex or can't afford it yet, go for one of the many other options. You can buy mattresses made entirely of organic cotton, mildew- and mold-resistant hemp, soy blends, castor beans, and antiallergy and antimicrobial bamboo.

# Pillows

Oh, the assorted horrors of synthetic pillows. No one will want to spend any time in your bedroom if you keep an eco-travesty at the head of your bed. Your delicate face and mucous membranes don't have to breathe in the chemicals off-gassing from conventional, petrochemically produced pillows. If you can't afford to make an investment in an eco-bed, you should at least consider one of the following eco-pillow options.

If you're a memory foam addict and love your ergonomic neck pillow, consider a natural latex pillow in a similar shape. It conforms to the contours of your body and supports the cervical spine. Another plus is that latex is antimicrobial and resists dust mites, so allergy-prone types will respond well to these. If you find that the pillow runs hot (as latex tends to do), try looking for one with venting holes.

The Rolls-Royce of eco-friendly, ergonomic pillows is the $O_2$ pillow, made by European Sleep Works in Berkeley, California (sleepworks.com). Beyond being made from Oeko-Tex certified latex foam and fabric, it's got a lot more going for it. The $O_2$ pillow maintains proper spinal support and opens airways for easier breathing and expanded lung capacity during sleep.

Why is this important? Oxygen deprivation during sleep causes a whole host of health issues, especially for those who snore or have sleep apnea. (Neither of these afflictions is very sexy.) The associated problems include headaches, daytime sleepiness, lethargy, shortened attention span, impaired judgment, depression, memory loss, weight gain, and increased risk of heart attack or stroke.

**Hemp** can be made into a pillow filling that has a tuft and feel similar to that of cotton pillows. They get softer with use. It's also mold resistant and not terribly fluffy. Some people are into that.

**Wool** pillows are great for wicking away moisture, and they're totally durable. (They're not for vegans, however.)

**Kapok** fiber might remind you of silk, but it'll last a lot longer. It's also great for allergies.

**Buckwheat** pillows are popular in Asia and used by those prone to back pain, migraines, muscle aches, stress, sleep apnea, and snoring. Buckwheat hulls are nice and cool around the head.

**Millet** isn't just for cereal. It has a high silicic acid content and, as a pillow, is thought to potentially stimulate the metabolism, soothe muscle pain, and heal the immune system. You can also look for green linens, blankets, comforters, nonallergenic pillows, and organic mattress covers all made from millet.

## Bed Linens

What about swaddling your happy, healthy mattress and pillows in equally eco-friendly fibers? Forget about Egyptian cotton and thread count. Look for certification from either IFOAM, Oeko-Tex, or other certifying agencies when shopping for linens.

**Amenityhome.com** makes exquisitely designed bedding. The duvet covers are made from organic cotton and printed with a limited-edition large-scale image; pillows are made from hemp and gorgeously printed as well. It's bed art. The company uses nontoxic water-based dyes and is certified by Control Union.

**Turninglife.com**, a company that practices zero-carbon shipping, carries a nice selection of certified organic cotton bedding, including blankets, comforters, shams, and pillowcases.

**Rawganique.com**, **Gaiam.com**, and **VivaTerra.com** often have great sustainable bedding options.

## Bedroom Furniture and Other Decor

Your first choice should always be vintage furniture—it's the greenest of the green ways to decorate your boudoir. Try local secondhand stores, Craigslist, eBay, and even freecycling, if it's available in your area. If you must choose new bedroom furniture, aim to find pieces that are durable and look like they'll last forever. Try to buy local—find artisans and furniture makers from your community who source their materials from within two hundred miles if possible. Stay away from teak or mahogany bed platforms (these woods are endangered) and choose recycled wood or wood that is sustainably harvested, such as ponderosa pine or birch. Go for sustainable or reclaimed wood certified with any of the following certifications: Rainforest Alliance, MBDC C2C (Cradle-to-Cradle), or Rediscovered Wood. Bamboo is another great alternative for bedroom furniture. It's a fast-growing, renewable resource that's grown without pesticides. But it's not a tree—it's actually a hearty grass.

Watch the finishes on your furniture as well—conventional wood furniture is usually sealed with toxic glop. Look for the Greenguard label to ensure that your furniture won't off-gas into your lungs, your home, or a landfill at some point in the future.

# Mood Lighting

Some of us like to do it in the dark, others with the lights blazing: just make sure you do it green. Now that we know that efficient fluorescent lightbulbs are mercury-filled toxic time bombs, how do we green our lighting? Incandescent bulbs are still a bad choice. In fact, as of mid-2009, the European Union began officially phasing them out, and the United States will soon follow. Sharp will introduce some super sexy, eco-friendly LED lighting options to the Japanese market soon; they have built-in dimmers and actually change color. Hopefully we can get our hot little hands on them too. Until that time comes, compact fluorescents are still best—just find out how and where to recycle them locally, saving the landfill from mercury contamination.

## *Light My Fire*

A recent study has found that paraffin, the most common inexpensive candle wax, may be carcinogenic. We breathe in a toxic brew as the candle burns. It's also a petroleum product, so it was never green to begin with. Beeswax and vegetable oil candles are the best eco-friendly alternatives. Look for soy and non-GMO palm oil candles. Also avoid metal or lead wicks; alternatives are organic cotton and even hemp wicks. Watch out for candles that tout themselves as "natural"—some actually contain paraffin or stearic acid, an animal-derived ingredient from meat-packing plants. You can also make your own candles with your lover—craft time!

## Eco-Friendly Candle Companies

Here are some sources of eco-friendly candles for you and your hunka hunka burning love.

**A Scent of Scandal** (ascentofscandal.com): This Los Angeles-based candle line, created by brother and sister team Ari Solomon (a vegan activist) and Heather Brancaccio, features 100 percent soy wax candles with cotton wicks and cheeky names. "Walk of Shame" is a green bouquet of lavender, rose, and jasmine notes with a musky background, while "Threesome" is a mix of strawberry, blueberry, and raspberry.

**Rawganique** (rawganique.com): This company makes candles with soy wax and hemp wicks, as well as a large variety of other eco-friendly products for the home.

**Eco Candle Company** (ecocandleco.com): This Wisconsin-based company makes soy candles in mason jars and other countrified receptacles. Their motto is "Enjoy with clean lungs and a clear conscience."

**Linneas Lights** (linneaslights.com): Hand-poured and made in small batches, these soy wax candles use lead-free cotton wicks and come in a nice variety of sexy signature scents, including tuberose and black vanilla. Very seductive indeed.

If you really want to turn on your houseguests, consider getting your crib LEED certified. LEED is an internationally recognized green building certification system that applies to both commercial and residential buildings. So you can opt to greenify your current dwelling, or if you're in the market for a new place, try to find one that's already certified. (Visit usgbc.org.)

**Nohm** (nohmcandles.com): These lovely candles contain non-GMO, pesticide-free, biodegradable soy wax. Nohm's line of votives are best used in multiples to light the edges of hallways as a trail to the bedroom.

**Paddywax** (paddywax.com): This line of chic candles has an eco-friendly collection that uses soy-based inks, hemp twine, recycled paper, and a chlorine-free paper pulp box that is biodegradable in three to six months.

**Scandle** (abodycandle.com): These exceptionally fun and interactive soy candles aren't just for lighting the room. They are meant to be poured onto the body and used as massage oil.

# Shower Power:
# Getting Clean after Getting Dirty

The typical American uses about 35 gallons of hot water per day. So soaping up with your loved one makes perfect eco-sense, as long as those hot showers follow certain plumbing guidelines. Use a low-flow filter showerhead that conserves water. Water Lily's eco-friendly Rain Showerhead can save up to 2,700 gallons and $75 per year in water and utility bills. Check all your faucets, because one "minor" leak can waste upward of 2,000 gallons of water per year.

## What's Hiding in Your Water?

Medco Health Solutions reported that *half* of all insured Americans were on medications for chronic health conditions,[32] so it's not so surprising that these drugs are getting passed back around in our water systems via sewage. That's not even the worst of what's lurking in your H$_2$O. Chlorine gas and chlorine by-products such as trihalomethanes, chloroform, and many synthetic chemicals may become vaporized in hot shower water, making your bathroom an arena for concentrated toxic gases. About 180 years ago, scientists discovered chlorine's ability to kill bacteria while researching ways to eradicate typhoid. It was also used as a weapon in World War I. It attacks organic matter, and you, little pretty, are an organic being. Chlorine bonds to skin and hair, destroying the natural bacterial balance. We consistently inhale these gases during showers, and this may pose a long-term health risk. At the very least, it may lead to dryness, itching, flaking, and premature skin aging—not very sexy. An eco-friendly shower filter can make all the difference. Many shower filters help balance water pH for better sudsing with your partner. (Remember, save water by showering with a friend.) Greenfeet.com has some excellent options in this arena, including the Rainshow'r line. After using a filter for just a few weeks, you should find that your hair is silkier and your skin feels softer. Installing the filters takes but a minute and doesn't seem to interfere with water pressure. Most filters need to be replaced about every six months.

## Do Drop the Industrial Soap

The whole antibacterial thing has backfired on us. It's part of the reason bacteria keep getting stronger: we keep killing them, and they build resistance to our weapons of mass "de-scrubtion." Recent studies suggest that even mothers of young children should let them get a little bit grubby before attacking them with baby wipes—the little tykes need to build resistance to bacteria, and they won't if it doesn't get into their systems. It's even been shown that people who grow up with animals in the house are generally healthier and less prone to allergies. Certain antibacterial soaps contain methylisothiazolinone, a potentially allergenic, cytotoxic substance linked to nerve cell death. Triclosan is pretty scary too. This aquatic-ecosystems destroyer is registered with the Environmental Protection Agency as a pesticide. A pristine alternative is Dr. Bronner's castile soap (drbronner.com). It's not just for hippies anymore, darling. It's vegan-friendly, fair trade, and certified organic, and it comes in a wide array of scents, even sexy ones like rose, lavender, and almond. A bonus is that this wonder soap can be used to wash your hair, clothes, or countertops.

## The Beauty, the Splendor, the Wonder of Your Hair

There are tons of excellent options for enviro-friendly hair care. As mentioned in chapter 3, John Masters is the master of truly earth-friendly shampoo, conditioner, and styling products. Do you blow-dry your hair? If you can give up your diffuser, you should—it's a waste of energy and your hair will be healthier if you forgo the heat. A nice little nighttime trick for women with long, straight hair is to wash, towel dry, and braid your locks. Make the braids looser or tighter depending on the look you want in the morning. You wake in the morning, and voilà—pain-free and heat-free styling. If you must use a blow-dryer, check out the Babar Ceramic ECO 8000, which claims to be radiation free and actually does seem to dry hair faster. But you can decide for yourself.

# It's Curtains for You

Vinyl shower curtains are as dangerous as they are ubiquitous. They have that telling "new car smell"—which simply means they're off-gassing like a herd of cows after a meal of baked beans. Typical vinyl shower curtains made of PVC contain the phthalate DEHP, linked to hormonal disruption in humans. This isn't what you want to inhale or absorb into your wet skin. The Virginia-based Center for Health, Environment and Justice commissioned a study about vinyl shower curtains, released in 2008. It found that these curtains were full of very frightening and dangerous substances, including 108 VOCs, some of which are listed by the EPA as air pollutants (toluene, ethyl-benzene, phenol, methyl isobutyl ketone, xylene, acetophenone, and cumene). Big-box stores have claimed they will phase this stuff out, but that's yet to occur. Organic cotton and hemp are your best alternatives. Be warned that hemp takes a long time to dry, so it may be better for hotter, dryer climates, because it tends to get moldy.

# Toweling Off

Once you step out of the shower, make sure that you dry off with environmentally friendly, body-loving towels. Wet hair and bodies do not look favorably upon towels made from conventional cotton, coated with pesticides and insecticides, and colored with chemical dyes. Many companies make beautiful, high-end, earth-friendly alternatives. Look for brands that have been certified by Oeko-Tex, the international gold standard of textile certification. Remember, however, the caveats about eco-friendly fibers discussed in chapter 3. There is no perfect choice. Bamboo gets high points in this category, since it's a renewable and biodegradable resource that doesn't require pesticides. Bamboo also feels like silk on the skin, and it's superabsorbent and antimicrobial. (Just note the differences in bamboo manufacturers before you buy.) Look for towels made with low-impact dyes. Organic cotton looks and feels great, it won't leach dyes or pesticides into your system, and you can feel good about the fact that farmworkers and soil aren't damaged by its production. Hemp is an excellent alternative, and it's very durable. It's not as plush as organic cotton, but it's a favorite in high-end, eco-friendly spas because it lasts forever.

## Speaking of Dirty . . .

Clean your bedroom, your bathroom, and the rest of your home with green cleaning products. DIY is easy here: baking soda and vinegar are two go-to cleaning options that cost little and purify a lot. There are a ton of cleaning products on the market, and, not surprisingly, this is one area in which greenwashing is rampant, so choose carefully. Avoid antibacterial types and make sure your product isn't petroleum-based. Here are some green cleaning supply brands of note:

**Biokleen** (biokleenhome.com)

**Ecover** (ecover.com)

**Seventh Generation** (seventhgeneration.com)

**20 Mule Team** (20muleteamlaundry.com)

For trash that can't be recycled, you can at least dispose of it in biodegradable plastic bags. BioBags (biobagusa.com) makes 100 percent biodegradable and compostable bags in every size imaginable.

**Nandina** (nandina.info) makes gorgeous, soft, hypoallergenic, absorbent, and decadent-feeling towels made from a blend of organic cotton and bamboo in an assortment of lovely colors that will make your bathroom very sexy indeed. These towels are loomed in a wind-powered factory, and they use only natural and low-impact dyes. Almond pearl, the company's natural fabric color, is pretty even though it's dye free. Nandina also makes incredibly plush bathrobes that make you say "Ahh."

**Dreamsacks** (dreamsacks.com) makes ribbed bamboo towels that are incredibly plush and soft. They're made with 70 percent bamboo and 30 percent organic cotton.

**Greenfeet** (greenfeet.com) carries a nice selection of organic cotton towels.

**Coyuchi** (coyuchi.com) offers towels and other goods made from organic cotton certified by IFOAM.

**Rawganique** (rawganique.com) sells organically grown European hemp terry-cloth towels. (Towels manufactured in China have issues with both human rights and chemical use.)

**VivaTerra** (vivaterra.com) carries both certified organic cotton and bamboo bath towels.

So you met your eco-mate, greened your bedroom, got dirty (while practicing safe sex, of course), and got clean again. Feels so good, right? But what if things went wrong (or right) and you are a soon-to-be a new parent? There's an eco-mom movement just waiting for you to sign up.

# CHAPTER ELEVEN

# THE ECO-PARENTING MOVEMENT: NOW THAT YOU'RE PLUS ONE, YOU'D BETTER MAKE GREEN YOUR MANTRA

*Kids. They're not easy.*
*But there has to be some penalty for sex.*
—Bill Maher

So, you had sex and now you're plus one (or more). From this point on, leading a sustainable lifestyle is no longer just a choice; it's something you must do in order to provide a safe and happy life for your little one(s). Awareness of how environmental degradation endangers the next generation is building, and parents are taking action locally and globally. A new movement centered on green parenting is gaining nationwide traction. The EcoMom Alliance is an organization dedicated to this movement. The alliance offers social networking and trains EcoMom leaders in communities all over the world. Their motto is "Sustain your self, sustain your home, sustain your world." Eco-parents have their work cut out for them, because babies and children face an increasingly toxic world in which even their bottles and toys are not safe.

# A Different Kind of Life Cycle Assessment

Let's begin at the beginning. Before baby comes pregnancy. And if you're preggers, your body and the one you're carrying in your uterus are very vulnerable to what's out there. If anyone should have eco-angst, it's a mom-to-be (or an overprotective dad-to-be). But don't freak out and give yourself or your soon-to-be-spawn an anxiety disorder. There is much you can do to mitigate the hazards.

## Body Burden: The Pollution in Newborns

Scientists once thought that the placenta protected the baby from pollutants. But in 2005, the Environmental Working Group and Commonweal did a benchmark investigation of industrial chemicals, pollutants, and pesticides in umbilical cord blood, and what they found was quite disturbing. The researchers found an average of 200 industrial chemicals and pollutants in umbilical cord blood from ten babies born in August and September of 2004 in U.S. hospitals. Tests revealed a total of 287 chemicals in the group. The umbilical cord blood of these ten children, collected by the Red Cross after the cord was cut, harbored pesticides, consumer product ingredients, and wastes from burning coal, gasoline, and garbage.[33]

This is scary stuff, but don't feel like you need to lock yourself in a climate-controlled chamber and grow hydroponic vegetables in order to survive the next nine months. You can take action to protect your baby. Let's start with what you need to avoid.

**Raw meat:** You really don't want to contract toxoplasmosis, coliform bacteria, or salmonella, so stay away from raw meat and even sushi for now.

**Deli meat:** Hello, *Listeria*. Deli meat is crawling with potential hazards to those with child (and frankly it's pretty gross even if you don't have a bun in your oven).

**Liver:** Liver contains a lot of vitamin A, which is thought to be dangerous to pregnant women in high doses. Skip the pâté.

**Fish with mercury:** Cross swordfish, shark, king mackerel, fresh tuna, sea bass, and tilefish off your to-eat list. You can sneak in a little canned tuna, but buy organic and don't consume more than 12 ounces in a week. (Note: If you dig fish and don't want to give it up entirely during your pregnancy, carry around the Monteray Bay Aquarium's "Seafood Watch Pocket Guide," mentioned in chapter 4.)

**Fish exposed to industrial pollutants:** Contaminated lakes and rivers are known to affect bluefish, striped bass, salmon, pike, trout, and walleye, like that three-eyed fish from *The Simpsons*. As long as you aren't fishing in local rivers and lakes, this probably isn't a concern for you.

**Raw shellfish:** Oysters, clams, and mussels, no matter how tempting, should probably be avoided for now. Even if cooked, they're still potentially dangerous to you and your fetus.

**Raw eggs:** Skip the freshly made Caesar salad, homemade mayonnaise, unpasteurized eggnog, homemade ice cream or custards, and hollandaise.

**Soft and blue cheeses:** More *Listeria* issues here. You may wake up in the middle of the night craving Brie, but don't go there. *Listeria* can cross the placenta and be life threatening. Say no to Camembert, Roquefort, feta, Gorgonzola, and Mexican cheeses like queso blanco and queso fresco.

**Unpasteurized milk:** Raw milk may well have benefits, but not for you, Ms. Mommypants.

**Caffeine:** Sorry, lady, you may be dying for a cuppa, but most sources say caffeine should be avoided during pregnancy. Some studies say it can be consumed in moderation, but you may just want to wait until the second trimester to indulge. If you can't give it up, make sure you don't have more than 300 mg of caffeine per day. Since it's a diuretic, it contributes to calcium loss, and you really need calcium right now. Try to drink tons of water and fresh juices instead. If you simply must get a fix of something that reminds you of coffee, try Cafix, a coffee substitute available at your local health food store.

**Alcohol:** French chicks do it, but you probably shouldn't. Having one or two glasses of wine during your pregnancy won't kill you, but it's not worth the potential risk to your little one. Absolutely avoid hard liquor all the way until you are done nursing. And no more keg stands, honey.

**Unwashed vegetables:** Scrub your veggies and rinse them like crazy or risk getting toxoplasmosis.

**Herbal remedies:** If you're working with a midwife or a doula, listen to her advice when it comes to herbs. Goldenseal, mugwort, and pennyroyal are all associated with miscarriage.

# Sex Tips for Pregnant Chicks

Just thinking about your precious cargo and how to care for it is an entirely exhausting endeavor. Do not, however, neglect one very important and wonderful fact about your life for the next nine months. You don't have to worry about getting pregnant! The stress that comes with birth control is temporarily on hold, and that's certainly good for the libido. And if you're preggers, you probably already know a secret that moms don't often share: you're horny as hell a lot of the time. It's because of all those crazy hormones churning around inside of you. If you're not in the middle of a bout of morning sickness, having back pain, or belching up a storm, you might fancy a throw-down, so your partner had better be ready to perform.

Many women report that sex during pregnancy is a revelation. You can do it all the way until birth, in most cases. Talk to your doc first, of course—sometimes a doctor will prescribe no sex because of specific conditions. (Bleeding is one reason that practitioners sometimes put a halt to getting busy.) If your doctor gives you the green light, go for it, knowing that orgasms are good for your baby—the rush of oxytocin may create a sense of euphoria for both of you. (Don't worry, the little one won't know what you're doing.) Masturbation and oral sex are also fine during pregnancy (just make sure nobody blows air into your vagina). Anal sex can become problematic toward the end of pregnancy because the baby's head pushes into the pelvis, so keep this in mind.

Pregnant sex is hot, but it can also present new challenges. If you're getting so huge that you can't figure out how to get it on, experiment with positions. Woman on top is a good, fun solution. If that doesn't work (or you're not feeling up to that much movement) try spooning. And, of course, good old doggie style keeps the pressure off your belly, although toward the end of pregnancy it may be harder to hold yourself up.

Here's a wonderful little factoid: orgasms sometimes come more easily to pregnant women. Even some formerly inorgasmic women are able to make it happen while with child because of the presence of additional fluids.

# After the Baby Arrives

Congratulations! You are now the proud parent of an adorable little person, which means you are entering the wild world of diapers, bottles, baby baths, and sleep deprivation. Because you're an eco-responsible parent, let's look at the healthiest options for said diapers, bottles, and bath-time products.

## The Diaper Debate

The debate about the merits of disposable diapers versus cloth goes on, but conventional disposal diapers are bad news on just about every level. In the United States alone, 18 billion diapers go into landfills every year, adding up to 82,000 tons of plastics and 1.3 million tons of wood pulp. Disposable diapers do not biodegrade because of the waterproof outer layer. Human waste is not supposed to be dumped in landfills—this is illegal—but with diapers, the issue is skirted. Some recent studies have suggested that the washing and drying cycles necessitated by the use of cloth diapers cancel out the bad environmental effects of disposables. Others have found potential health issues lurking in disposable diapers because of the crystals used to make them absorbent.

But it's certain that unbleached organic cotton diapers are the lowest-impact diaper option available at this time. Diaperjungle.com is a one-stop shop with answers to all your questions about cloth diapers.

BumGenius diapers are one-size-fits-all cloth diapers with a twist: you don't have to keep buying new sets as your baby grows, and the disposable cotton insert isn't dangerous to your baby's tush or to the environment.

Bamboo is also an option. With all the great things you know about bamboo, why wouldn't you want it for a diaper? As long as the fibers haven't been treated with chemicals, this is an excellent alternative to conventional diapers. BumGenius also offers a bamboo fitted diaper in addition to those mentioned above.

## Bottle Beware!

You're probably considering breast-feeding, but unless you plan to be the only person feeding your baby, you'll need to have a few bottles on hand so your partner or sitter can take a shift while you get a well-deserved break. The materials used to make plastic baby bottles have recently come under fire, so choose carefully.

Bisphenol A, a chemical used to make polycarbonate, is widely used in baby bottles and is a very scary thing you don't want in your growing child's body. According to an organization called Environment California, bisphenol A is a developmental, neural, and reproductive toxin that has been linked to cancer, impaired immune function, early onset of puberty, obesity, and diabetes, even in small doses. In bottles, it is thought to leach into the liquid they hold. *Consumer Reports* did a study in 1999 that found bisphenol A leached into formula during the heating process used to sterilize bottles for infants.

Amazingly, the FDA stands by its approval of polycarbonate baby bottles. But who wants to take that chance?

The safest alternative? Glass. Although some mothers find it less convenient, it's a nontoxic option that lasts for a long time and can be handed down to new generations of babies. And it can always be recycled. Nurture Pure, BornFree, and Evenflo all make glass bottles. If you're not into glass, search out bisphenol A–free bottles from companies like Adiri, Green to Grow, Dr. Brown's, and Medela.

## Rubber Ducky, You're the One

It turns out that bath time may not be so much fun. Remember those Johnson & Johnson commercials about their gentle and pure shampoo? Turns out, not so much. Baby bath products, including shampoo, soap, bubble baths, and baby lotions are full of poisons that you most certainly don't want anywhere near your baby. According to a report by the Campaign for Safe Cosmetics, "Formaldehyde and 1,4-dioxane are known carcinogens; formaldehyde can also trigger skin rashes in some children. Unlike many other countries, the U.S. government does not limit formaldehyde, 1,4-dioxane, or most other hazardous substances in personal care products."[34] In 2009, the campaign delivered a letter to Johnson & Johnson's chief executive officer asking that the company reformulate its personal care products to ensure they are free of 1,4-dioxane and to phase out phthalates. They also asked the company to reformulate its products to avoid the use of quaternium-15 and other formaldehyde-releasing preservatives, and to switch to safer preservatives. As of the publishing of this book, the Safe Baby Products Act, meant to force the FDA to properly regulate baby personal care products, had been introduced in Congress but had not yet been made into law. In the meantime, use personal care products from clean, green companies like California Baby, Erbaviva, Weleda, Earth Mama Angel Baby, and Balm Balm for irritated tushies.

## A Baby on Board Needn't Mean Sex Is Off Limits

Mom's exhausted from carrying a kid for nine long months, neither Mom nor Dad has gotten a wink of sleep in weeks, and both of you are in no mood for love. How do you keep the flame lit when you're covered in baby vomit, have sore nipples, and feel like your baby weight isn't going anywhere? For new moms, getting a few hours alone to decompress and feel human again is the best sexual stimulant, period. Have your partner watch the tyke and take a yoga class or catch a spa break, even if just for an hour.

Next, even if it seems impossible, plan at least one night a week for a date—even if it's a date in the living room. That means turning off your respective Blackberries, shutting your laptops, and tuning out the world. It helps if the landline stays off the hook for a few hours too. Add a touch of eco-friendly candlelight and an organic dinner

### Go-To Green Mom Blogs

Eco-mommies have practically taken over the Internet. Here are a few of their best blogs and e-commerce sites.

ecochildsplay.com

greenbabyguide.com

greenmomhappymom.com

greenmoms.com

teensygreen.com

thegreenmomreview.com

(take-out is fine if neither of you has time to cook these days). Even carving out two hours of time for emotional intimacy can bring back the sexual spark that's been drowned out by wet diapers and hourly feedings. Even if you're not ready for sex yet, try making out on the couch or just cuddling in front of the TV. Women shouldn't feel like they have to jump back in and perform acrobatically after nine months (and more) of devoting their entire body and soul to another being. And men shouldn't feel rejected if their partners aren't ready. Just don't fall into that cliché "no sex after baby" trap. If you can keep emotional and spiritual intimacy alive, you'll eventually get back to the sex life that you were once accustomed to.

## First Comes Love, Then Comes Green Marriage

If all the hot sex you've been having has led to the bond of a lifetime, take it to the next level with green nuptials. The traditional wedding industry is notoriously wasteful. The worst offender? Destination weddings. All the jet fuel used to get your friends and family to that island in the Caribbean is not worth all the bad carbon karma. So go local. The more people you invite, the wider your footprint, so opt for a more intimate affair and list public transportation on the invite. For the invitations, look to paper and printing companies using recycled or otherwise eco-friendly materials. If you want green gifts, register at a site like Gaiam.com. Look for organic, sustainable caterers, and don't let the conventions of a wedding planner's little black book limit your scope. Order flowers from local, sustainable growers. Make sure your wedding dress is made from the right stuff and adorn your bridesmaids in dresses that they'll actually want to wear again. Consider honeymooning locally, travel by train, or opt for (non-greenwashed) eco-tourism.

# Burning up for your love

*Sex is not the answer. Sex is the question.*
*"Yes" is the answer.*

—Swami X

You're going to have sex no matter what, so why not do it right? If you've been reluctant to green your lifestyle because it seemed too complicated or even cliché, now you see why eco-sexuality is a seductive bridge to all things green. You don't have to do it for some far-off, amorphous reason that you can't wrap your brain around. You can simply do it because you want your sex life to maintain its sizzle while keeping the planet cool. And with all the fringe benefits of eco-sex (health, stamina, increased sensuality, and consciousness expansion), how could you possibly pass it up?

Just remember that greenwashers and climate-change deniers are as bad as those lecherous, seedy types you see in bars—the ones you wouldn't go home with under any circumstance. You know them when you see 'em. Learn to do the same thing when approached by corporations that want to get into your pants. Turn them down and move on to something better. Consumer-led trends and boycotts are even more effective in the age of blogging and social media, so we're actually getting ahead of the game right now. Eco-sexuals are far more sophisticated than most. Use that empowerment and use it well.

You may not be president or even a green technology entrepreneur, but you can make a big difference. You don't have to take global warming lying down (unless, of course, that's your preferred position). The ravages of climate change should be a powerful inducement to act. Unless you have buried your head in the sand and are going on your merry way ignoring all the signs, you know it in your mind and gut. In his opening remarks to the United Nations Climate Change Summit in 2009, secretary Ban Ki-moon told the dignitaries and world leaders, "Now is the moment to act in common cause. History may not offer us a better chance." We need to feel the urgency of this pivotal historical moment as much as we feel the urgency of our loins. You've got to want to save the planet as much as you want to get laid.

# The Ultimate Carbon Offset: Remaining Childless by Choice

*If we don't halt population growth with justice and compassion, it will be done for us by nature, brutally and without pity—and will leave a ravaged world.*
—Nobel Laureate Dr. Henry W. Kendall

Our culture adores its mommies. Witness our obsession with Angelina Jolie and her brood, and the media's fascination with celebrity "baby bumps." We glamorize motherhood in increasingly unhealthy ways. In 2008 and 2009, an explosion of multiple babies seemed to take over our televisions: we had both the Octomom and *Jon & Kate Plus 8.* (It seemed at one point that every show on the Learning Channel was about families with inordinate amounts of children.) Motherhood is seen as a status symbol; even National Public Radio profiled the "competitive birthing" trend in 2007. But in the midst of all our baby making, a quiet revolution is emerging.

Without fanfare, more and more people are choosing to have great sex that doesn't result in kids. Some couples make this decision because they're committed to a greener world, and some do it for a whole host of other reasons, both personal and political. In Laura S. Scott's recent book *Two Is Enough: A Couple's Guide to Living Childless by Choice*, she chronicles men and women who have made the conscious decision not to have children. They may define themselves as "child free" or "childless," but they shouldn't be ashamed of their choices. Some of her interviewees had to go through a painful process to find acceptance from their family and friends. Society puts tremendous pressure on young couples, particularly heterosexual ones, to have kids. (Gay couples, ironically, deal with the exact opposite—when they want to adopt or hire a surrogate, they have to jump through hoops.) It's not just would-be grandparents, but colleagues, friends with children, and the culture at large that compel even those who are ambivalent about children to have them. Scott discovered that some of the people she interviewed were so influenced by cultural and familial pressure that they weren't even aware that they had a choice in the matter—they assumed they would simply grow up, get married, and have kids, because that's just what you do.[35]

Imagine how many people secretly wonder if parenthood is right for them but decide to do it anyway. Children born into an atmosphere of doubt and regret often suffer the most. Not that all ambivalent parents fail to love their children—we all know someone who was an "accident" but turned out to be the best thing that ever happened to his or her parents. But still, we'd all benefit from thinking about this serious subject in advance instead of mindlessly doing what seems "natural." In the end, social pressure may have far more to do with our need to breed. Florida State University professor Robin Simon did a study that found parents are more depressed than those without children—even after their kids have left the nest.[36] Perhaps this is because they didn't choose to have kids with full consciousness; maybe they did it because it seemed like their only choice.

Some people are born, as Joseph Campbell says, to "follow their bliss." When that bliss doesn't include biological children, people shouldn't be made to feel like freaks. It's thirty-somethings who feel the most pressure, but any childless person in his or her childbearing years will eventually hear the question "So when are you having kids?" Super sexy environmentalist Cameron Diaz had this to say to *Cosmopolitan UK* in 2009, "I think women are afraid to say they don't want children or they're going to get shunned."[37] It's incredibly controversial, but it must be said out loud.

Some women focus on their career and postpone childbearing, and then find themselves in a biological-clock panic in their late thirties. Some freeze their eggs, undergo fertility treatments, or hire surrogates. For some, this choice is the right one; for others, it's a road paved with regret and frustration. Costly, time-consuming, and sometimes painful fertility treatments end up in multiple births at least 20 percent of the time, according to a recent article in the *New York Times*.[38] Many of these babies are born premature, and their mothers are often ridden with health problems.

It's hard to even discuss remaining childless by choice until the playing field is truly leveled for everyone who *does* want to have a child, whether biological or adopted. For now, gay couples and single would-be parents face struggles that married, heterosexual couples do not. Until this paradigm shifts and everyone who truly wants children can have equal access to adoption, those who remain childless by choice will be one marginalized group among many.

## Population Out of Hand

On Human Rights Day in 1967 the United Nations issued a statement about overpopulation that became the touchstone for a fiery "zero population growth" movement. This rising awareness also led to overzealous leaders who championed contraception and, in some cases, enforced sterilization. China's one-child policy was adopted in the late 1970s and Birth Planning Commissioners did what they thought they had to do.

Despite the uncompromising, radical zeal that accompanied this movement, we can't forget that overpopulation is truly a problem on our planet. We tend to think of the overpopulation that occurs in the third world, but a child born in the United States has more than 160 times the impact on the planet as a Bangladeshi child, if you add in potential descendants. Zero population growth in this country could actually be a good idea. However, contemporary environmentalists, if they want to change hearts and minds, should take an entirely different tack from the one taken in the 1970s. People shouldn't be made to feel guilty for wanting kids. But if baby making is something they're already questioning privately, then they should be armed with all the facts and empowered to make their own decision.

According to Laura Scott, "Most people living in North America are, or will become, parents. The decision not to have children remains exceptional. Even today, when marriage is increasingly optional, the idea that kids are optional, too has yet to be entertained by the majority." It's time for us to start having the discussion.

# Adoption: A Greener Choice?

You already know the inherent issues involved in increasing your carbon legacy. If you adopt instead of producing a biological child, you can be a part of reversing that trend while actually *saving* a life and enriching your own. Adoption advocates estimate that, by 2017, 250 million children will be in need of adoptive families.[39] On the other hand, a recent article by E. J. Graff in *Foreign Policy* suggests that international adoption industry statistics are grossly inflated. According to Graff, hundreds of thousands of children do need homes, but they are not the healthy infants most Westerners want to adopt—they are often older than five and some are sick or disabled. Fraud has grown rampant because of the fervor of the marketplace. Western families desperately want babies, and the industry supplies them, at great cost, and sometimes without the actual consent of their biological parents.[40] Despite this controversy, eco-sexuals shouldn't give up on adoption as an alternative to having biological children. We simply must change the rules if we want to create a world in which adoption is transparent, free of fraud, and not cost-prohibitive.

Adoption is currently a very expensive and time-consuming process that requires patience, dedication, and savings. Adopting within the United States also presents many problems, from the condition of children in foster care (where drug and other abuse is rampant among the biological mothers of children in need of care), to extremely long waits that can end up being futile, since birth mothers often change their minds. If enough people decide that they're going to adopt rather than have biological children, it should eventually become easier to adopt. The billion-dollar fertility industry has been scrutinized in recent years for its questionable ethics, and it may be time for baby-hungry couples (or singles) to reconsider the need to produce genetic replicas when so many beautiful babies already need their love. (Another option is to have one child biologically and adopt the other. Even that will reduce your carbon footprint considerably and make one lonely child extremely happy.) Environmentalists and adoption advocates should come together and realize that their movements are inextricably linked.

If you love kids but don't think having one is right for you, then consider helping one of the many children in your community who needs you right now. You can teach, volunteer, mentor, babysit, or be a really awesome aunt or uncle. Without all the pressure of being a parent, you can still get all the pleasure of spending time with tiny humans. They are pretty damn miraculous to be around, even if they don't share your genes.

Whatever you choose, know that, with the population of the planet headed toward the nine-billion mark by the middle of the twenty-first century, eco-sexuals really can help save the world.

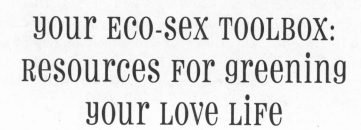

# уouʀ ᴇᴄо-ѕᴇх ᴛооʟʙох: ʀᴇѕоuʀᴄᴇѕ ꜰоʀ ɢʀᴇᴇɴɪɴɢ уоuʀ ʟоⱱᴇ ʟɪꜰᴇ

## Books

### Sustainability/Environment

Carson, Rachel. *Silent Spring.* New York: Houghton Mifflin, 1962.

Doppelt, Bob. *The Power of Sustainable Thinking.* London: Earthscan Books, 2008.

Goleman, Daniel. *Ecological Intelligence.* New York: Broadway Books, 2009.

Gore, Al. *Our Choice: A Plan to Solve the Climate Crisis.* New York: Rodale Press, 2009.

McDonough, William. *Cradle to Cradle.* New York: North Point Press, 2002.

# Sex

Carrellas, Barbara. *Urban Tantra: Sacred Sex for the Twenty-first Century.* Berkeley: Celestial Arts, 2007.

Michaels, Mark A., Patricia Johnson, and Tristan Taormino. *Tantra for Erotic Empowerment: The Key to Enriching Your Sexual Life.* Woodbury, MN: Llewellyn Publications, 2008.

Moalem, Sharon. *How Sex Works: Why We Look, Smell, Taste, Feel, and Act the Way We Do.* New York: Harper, 2009.

Roach, Mary. *Bonk: The Curious Coupling of Science and Sex.* New York: W. W. Norton, 2008.

Weschler, Toni. *Taking Charge of Your Fertility: The Definitive Guide to Natural Birth Control, Pregnancy Achievement, and Reproductive Health.* New York: Harper, 2006.

# Food (Gardening, Ethics, Diet, and Preserving)

Bartholomew, Mel. *All New Square Foot Gardening.* Franklin, TN: Cool Springs Press, 2005.

Foer, Jonathan Safran. *Eating Animals.* New York, Little Brown, 2009.

Fried, Robert, and Lynn Edlen-Nezin. *Great Food, Great Sex: The Three Food Factors for Sexual Fitness.* New York: Ballantine Books, 2006.

Lindberg, Marrena. *The Orgasmic Diet: A Revolutionary Plan to Lift Your Libido and Bring You to Orgasm.* New York: Crown Publishing, 2007.

Petrini, Carlo. *Slow Food Nation.* New York: Rizzoli Ex Libris, 2007.

Ruppenthal, R. J. *Fresh Food from Small Spaces.* White River Junction, VT: Chelsea Green, 2008.

Silverstone, Alicia, *The Kind Diet: A Simple Guide to Losing Weight, Feeling Great, and Saving the Planet.* New York: Rodale Books, 2009.

## Sustainable Cities

Kellogg, Scott, and Stacy Pettigrew. *Toolbox for Sustainable City Living.* Cambridge: South End Press, 2008.

Owen, David. Green Metropolis: *Why Living Smaller, Living Closer, and Driving Less are the Keys to Sustainability.* New York: Riverhead Books, 2009.

# The Eco-Sexual Online

## General Eco

350.org

beyondtalk.net

envirolink.org

greenpeace.org

grist.org

inhabitat.com

lifegoggles.com

sustainabilitydictionary.com

treehugger.com

## Lifestyle

inhabitat.com

strawberryearth.com

thedailygreen.com

thelazyenvironmentalist.com

## DIY Sources

essentialwholesale.com

mountainroseherbs.com

## Environmental Product Ratings

cosmeticsdatabase.com

ecolabelling.org

fairtrade.net

goodguide.com

## Green/Environmental Consulting

Green Irene: greenirene.com

Green Living Consulting: greenlivingconsulting.com

Patrick J. Duffy, MRP, AICP: pjdgreenecon.net

## Food

cleanplatesnyc.com

rawfoods.com

seedsofchange.com

slowfood.com

sustainabletable.com

theppk.com (PostPunkKitchen)

vegetariantimes.com

## Animals and Veganism

caringcconsumer.com

farmsanctuary.org

peta.org

supervegan.com

vegan.org

veganoutreach.org

## Fashion and Beauty

eco-chick.com

ecofabulous.com

ecofashionworld.com

ecostiletto.com

ecouterre.com

etsy.com

thegreenloop.com

## Sex

badvibes.org

blog.babeland.com

eartherotics.com

ecosex.ca

edenfantasys.com/sexis

nerve.com

smittenkittenonline.com

vegporn.com

## Sexologists/Sexperts

Dan Savage: thestranger.com/
seattle/SavageLove

Jamye Waxman: jamyewaxman.com

Rachel Kramer Bussel: lustylady
.blogspot.com

Tracey Cox: traceycox.com

Violet Blue: tinynibbles.com

## Other Eco-Sexy People, Places, and Things

avaaz.org

babycakesnyc.com

bryant-terry.com

crazysexylife.com

ecogeek.org

ecorazzi.com

girliegirlarmy.com

noimpactman.typepad.com

oneluckyduck.com

thediscerningbrute.com

thegroovymind.com

theyesmen.org

# ENDNOTES

1. J. M. Broder. "Climate Change Seen as Threat to U.S. Security," *New York Times*, www.nytimes.com/2009/08/09/science/earth/09climate.html?_r=1 (accessed August 31, 2009).

2. *The Dictionary of Sustainable Management*, "Sustainability," www.sustain abilitydictionary.com/s/sustainability.php (accessed September 6, 2009).

3. A. Costello, M. Abbas, and A. Allen. "Managing the Health Effects of Climate Change," *Lancet*, 373: 1693–1733.

4. P. A. Murtaugh, and M. G. Schlax. "Reproduction and the Carbon Legacies of Individuals," *Global Environmental Change* 19: 14–20.

5. *The Dictionary of Sustainable Management*, "Carbon Footprint," www.sustainabilitydictionary.com/c/carbon_footprint.php (accessed September 15, 2009).

6. Murtaugh, 14.

7. Environmental Working Group, "Human Toxome Project," www.ewg.org/sites/humantoxome/ (accessed August 15, 2009).

8. Environmental Working Group, "Phthalates," www.ewg.org/chemindex/term/480 (accessed September 2, 2009).

9. Coming Clean, "Body Burden," www.chemicalbodyburden.org/whatisbb.htm (accessed August 1, 2009).

10. Environmental Protection Agency, "Life Cycle Assessment," www.epa.gov/nmrl/lcaccess/ (accessed July 15, 2009).

11. Fairtrade Labelling Organizations International, "Fairtrade," www.fairtrade.net/standards.html (accessed August 4, 2009).

12. Reprinted by permission of TerraChoice Environmental Marketing, http://sinsofgreenwashing.org/findings/the-seven-sins/ (accessed June 15, 2009).

13. Environmental Working Group, *Skin Deep Cosmetic Safety Database*, www.cosmeticsdatabase.com/faq.php (accessed June 1, 2009).

14. Green America Today, "Green Business," www.greenamericatoday.org/greenbusiness/screening.cfm (accessed September 2, 2009).

15. Reprinted by permission of the Campaign for Safe Cosmetics, "The Compact for Safe Cosmetics," http://safecosmetics.org/article.php?id=341 (accessed June 1, 2009).

16. Campaign for Safe Cosmetics, "A Poison Kiss: The Problem of Lead in Lipstick," www.safecosmetics.org (accessed November 9, 2009).

17. *The Dictionary of Sustainable Management*, "Closed-loop Supply Chain," www.sustainabilitydictionary.com/c/closedloop_supply_chain.php (accessed November 20, 2009).

18. Farm Sanctuary, "FactoryFarming.com:Environmental Impact," www.farmsanctuary.org/issues/factoryfarming/environment/ (accessed September 14, 2009).

19. Vegan Outreach, "Environmental Destruction," www.veganoutreach.org/whyvegan/environment.html (accessed October 9, 2009).

20. Worldhealth.net, "Chocolate: A Boon for the Libido and the Heart," www.worldhealth.net/news/chocolate_a_boon_for_the_libido_and_the_ (accessed July 10, 2009).

21. International Rescue Committee, "Special Report: Congo," www.theirc.org/special-reports/special-report-congo-x (accessed December 9, 2009).

22. M. A. Ismail. "Spending on Lobbying Thrives," The Center for Public Integrity, http://projects.publicintegrity.org/rx/report.aspx?aid=823 (accessed December 9, 2009).

23. A. Gardner. "Joyful Music in Tune with Heart Health," *Health Day*, http://health.usnews.com/articles/health/healthday/2008/11/11/joyful-music-in-tune-with-heart-health.html (accessed December 10, 2009).

24. Green Music Alliance, www.greenmusicalliance.org (accessed July 18, 2009).

25. WebMD, "Drugs Linked to Erectile Disfunction," www.webmd.com/erectile-dysfunction/guide/drugs-linked-erectile-dysfunction (accessed August 17, 2009).

26. M. Kahn. "Horny Goat Weed May Offer Viagara Alternative," *Reuters*, www.reuters.com/article/oddlyEnoughNews/idUSTRE48T6WS20080930 (accessed August 5, 2009).

27. N. S. Rastogi. "Tree Humper: What's the Greenest Form of Birth Control?" *Slate* www.slate.com/id/2212648/ (accessed July 10, 2009).

28. *Immunology and Cell Biology* 75 (2), 190–192.

29. J. Weiss. "Best Supplements for Nutrient-Depleting Drugs," MSN Health and Fitness, http://health.msn.com/health-topics/articlepage.aspx?cp-documentid=100220332 (accessed August 31, 2009).

30. K. Sheppard, "15 Green Cities," *Grist*, www.grist.org/article/cities3.

31. Reprinted with permission of Coalition Against Toxic Toys, "Safe Toys Shopping Guid," http://badvibes.org/?p=12#more-12 (accessed August 28, 2009).

32. Medco, "Chronic Medication Nation: Research Finds Chronic Health Problems Now Afflict More than Half of All Americans," http://medco.mediaroom.com/index.php?s=43&item=317 (accessed June 2, 2009).

33. Environmental Working Group, "Body Burden: The Pollution in Newborns, www.ewg.org/reports/bodyburden2/execsumm.php (accessed August 14, 2009).

34. The Campaign for Safe Cosmetics, "No More Toxic Tub," www.safecosmetics.org/article.php?id=414 (accessed June 20, 2009).

35. L. S. Scott. *Two Is Enough: A Couple's Guide to Living Childless by Choice.* Berkeley: Seal Press, 2009.

36. R. K. Britt. "Kids Are Depressing, Studies of Parents Finds, *Live Science*, www.livescience.com/health/060207_parent_depression.html (accessed October 10, 2009).

37. *Cosmopolitan UK* (June 2009).

38. S. Saul. "Grievous Choice on Risky Path to Parenthood," *New York Times*, www.nytimes.com/2009/10/12/health/12fertility.html?scp=1&sq=fertility&st=cse (accessed October 15, 2009).

39. Sunrise Adoption, "News," www.sunriseadoption.com/adoptive_parents/news?page=2 (accessed August 14, 2009).

40. E. J. Graff. "The Lie We Love," Foreign Policy, www.foreignpolicy.com/story/cms.php?story_id=4508 (accessed November 30, 2009).

# inDex

## A

Abortion, 139–40
Adoption, 202–3
Agave-Sweetened Brownie Gems, 90–91
Alcohol, 190
Allergies, 121, 183
Amines, 19
Amorous Bath Oil, 35
Antibacterials, 20, 39, 61, 182–83, 185
Aphrodisiacs
    about, 75–76
    essential oils, 49–51
    more eco-foods, 92–93
    recipes for seducing a man, 77–84
    recipes for seducing a woman, 84–91
    seductive dessert, 90–91
Argan oil, 39–40
Arginine, 99, 111–12, 144–45
Aromatherapy, 46–47
Asparagus, 92
Asparagus and Sweet Potato Curry,
    86–87
Australian Organic Standard, 24

## B

Babies
    adopting, 202–3
    bathtime safety, 194–95
    bottles, 193–94
    diapers, 6, 192–93
    environmental impact of, 6–7
    pollution in newborns, 188–90
Baby powder, 20
Back pain, 175
Bamboo, 56–57, 178, 184–85, 186
Basal body temperature, 138
Bath oils, 35, 37
Bathtime
    baby's, 194–95
    showers, 181–86
BDIH, German certification
    agency, 24
Beauty standards, 28–29
Bed linens, 177–78
Bed mattress, 172–75
Bedroom, 171–81
*Better Sex Through Yoga*, 113–14

Birth control
    about, 128–29
    condoms, 1–2, 129–30, 163
    diaphragms and cervical caps, 133–34
    IUD, 135
    morning-after pill, 131
    natural, 136–39
    neem oil, 130–31
    pills, 2, 120, 132–33
    sponge, the, 134
    tying the tubes, 134–35
Bling, 105–6
Body burden, 9, 188–90
Body moisturizers, 40–41
Body scrubs, 36
Bone, Eugenia, 70
Breath fresheners, 41
Brown Sugar Body Scrub, 34–35
Buckwheat pillows, 177
Butterfly stretch, 116–17

## C

Caffeine, 190
California Certified Organic Farmers
    (CCOF), 22
Canadian Organic Standard, 23
Candles, 179–81
Carbon footprint, 7–8, 28–29, 110, 203
Cardamom-Saffron Sweet Lassi, 85
Carnal Cleanse, 124–25
Carrellas, Barbara, 157, 158
Cellulite, 42
Cervical caps, 133–34
Chanterelle and Yuzu Ceviche, 78–80
Childbirth, sex after, 195–96
Childless couples, 198–201
Children. See Babies
Chile peppers, 92

Chlamydia, 144
Chocolate
    about, 98–99
    Agave-Sweetened Brownie Gems,
      90–91
    aphrodisiac qualities, 90, 93
    Cacao Nib Shake, 83–85
    eco-friendly brands, 99–103
Cities, greenest, 150–52
Cleaning products, 185
Cleanse, carnal, 124–25
Cleansers, face and body, 37
Climate change, 2–3, 197, 198
Closed-loop system, 58, 59
Clothing
    dry-cleaning, 65
    green fabrics, 56–60, 63
    handbags, 64
    lingerie, 61–62
    mass-produced, 27–28
    shoes, 62–63
    shopping for, 64–66
    vintage, 55–56
Cocktail recipe, 82–83
Coconut oil, 39
Colors, synthetic, 20
Communication, 153–54
Compact for Safe Cosmetics, 22, 30–31
Condoms, 1–2, 129–30, 163
Consciousness, 13–14
Cooking tips, 92
Cookware, 92
Cork, 58–59
Cosmetics. See also Personal care
    products
    makeup, 42–44
    safety concerns, 27, 29–33
Cotton, organic, 57, 186

Cox, Janice, 33–35
Creamy Oats with a Crunch, 89–90
Curtains, shower, 184

# D

Damiana, 93
Dating, 32, 155–57
Demeter International, 25
Dessert, seductive, 90–91
Diamonds, 103–4
Diapers, 6, 192–93
Diaphragms, 133–34
*Dictionary of Sustainable Management*,
   7, 58
Dining, 93–94, 155–57
Doppelt, Bob, 4, 5
Dry-cleaning, 65
Duke, James, 122

# E

*EcoBeauty*, 33–35
ECOCERT, 24
*Ecological Intelligence*, 13, 25
Eco-sexuality
   choosing, 197
   overview, 3–4, 5
   websites, 206–7
Endorphins, 92, 112, 168
Energy Star certified, 17
Environmental consciousness, 13–14
Erectile dysfunction (ED), 117–18
Essential oils, aphrodisiacs, 49–51
Etsy.com, 60
European Standards, 23–24
Exercise, 112–17, 122
Eyeliner, 44
Eye moisturizers, 41–42
Eye shadow, 44

# F

Fabric, green, 56–60, 63
Face scrubs and cleansers, 36–37
Facial masks, 33–34, 38
Facial moisturizers, 39–40
Facial tissues, 17
Fair-trade, 14, 22
Feet moisturizers, 42
Fertility treatments, 200, 201
Fish/seafood, 75, 190
Flax linen fabric, 58
Flowers, 2, 96–98
Food. *See also* Aphrodisiacs
   to avoid during pregnancy, 189–90
   cooking tips, 92
   local, 69–70
   organic, 70–71
   overview, 67–68
   raw, 71
   seafood/fish, 75, 190
   slow food approach, 68–69
   vegan, 73–74
   vegetarian, 72–73
Forest Stewardship Council (FSC), 23
Formaldehyde, 17, 19, 172, 194
*Fresh Food from Small Spaces*, 70
Fruit detox, 124–25
Furniture, 178

# G

Gardening, 69–70
Genetically modified organisms
   (GMOs), 58, 59, 68, 111
Global warming, 2, 198
Gold, 104–5
Goleman, Daniel, 13, 25
GoodGuide.com, 13
Greaux, Jacquie Noelle, 113–14

Green America, 23

*Green Pharmacy Herbal Handbook, The*, 122

Greenseal, 22

Greenwashing, 11–13, 17–18, 30, 94, 197–98

## H

Hair products, 37–38, 183

Handbags, 64

Health. *See* Sexual health

Hemp, 57, 177, 184, 185

Herbs, 122, 138–39, 190

Herpes, 131, 144–45

Holistic thinking, 4–5

Honey Cap, 134

Horny goat weed, 126

Human Papillomavirus (HPV), 142

## I

IFOAM certification, 25

Ingeo fabric, 59

ISO (International Organization for Standardization), 23

IUD (intrauterine device), 135

## J

Japanese Agriculture Standard, 24

Jewelry, 103–6

## K

Kapok pillows, 177

Kegel exercises, 115, 122

## L

Langheld, Jennifer, 113–14

Latex, natural, 130, 173–74, 176

Leaping Bunny Program, 22

Libido, 76, 99, 118, 126, 171, 191

Libido-Stimulating Scent, 48

Life cycle assessment (LCA), 10–11

Lighting, 179–81

Lingerie, 61–62

Lip moisturizers, 41–42

Lipstick, 44

Liquor, 95

*Living Raw Food,* 75–76

Local foods, 69–70

Lubricants, 2, 145–46

Lyocell fabric, 59

## M

Makeup, 42–44

Mascara, 44

Masks, facial, 38

Massage oils, 52, 168–70

Mattress, 172–75

Medications, 120, 126

Melngailis, Sarma, 71, 75–76

Menopause, 121

Menstruation, 140–41

Millet pillows, 177

Mindfulness meditation, 116

Modal fabric, 59

Moisturizers, 39–42

Morning-After Breakfast, 83–85, 89–90

Morning-after pill, 131

Motherhood, 195, 198–201

Music, 110

## N

Nail polish, 20, 42

Nanoparticles, 21

Natural birth control, 136–39

*Natural Liberty*, 140

Neem oil, 130–31, 145

Networking, 148–49, 152

New Zealand's Official Organic
    Assurance Program (OOAP), 25
Nitric oxide (NO), 111
Nutrition, 111–12

## O

Off-gassing, 160, 163
Oil, 2, 3–4
Organic food, 70–71
Organizations, helpful, 21–25
Orgasms, 113, 118, 119, 158, 191, 192
Oysters, 93

## P

Parabens, 19, 32, 145, 146
Parenthood, 187–88, 199–200
Pelvic floor prolapse, 120, 122, 126
Pelvic inflammatory disease (PID),
    143–44
Pelvic stretching, 115–17
People for the Ethical Treatment of
    Animals (PETA), 22
Perfumes
    making your own, 47–52
    natural brands, 52–53
    synthetic, 30 45–47
Personal care products
    buying, 36–44
    making your own, 33–35
    safety concerns, 29–33
    toxic ingredients in, 18–21, 27
Peyronie's disease, 123, 127
Pharmaceutical industry, 109–10,
    117–18
Pheromones, 46
Phthalates, 9, 19, 30, 161–62, 194
Pillows, 176–77
Plastic, 3, 161
Plastic bags, biodegradable, 185

Population issues, 6–8, 198–99, 201–2
*Power of Sustainable Thinking, The*, 4, 5
Pregnancy, 7, 188–93
Premature ejaculation, 122, 123,
    126, 127
Propylene glycol, 20–21

## R

Raw food diet, 71
*Raw Food/Real World*, 75
Rayon, 59
Razors, 38
Recipes, 77–91
Restaurants, 93–94
Rhythm method, 136–37
Rich, Richie, 54
Ruppenthal, R.J., 70

## S

Sarma Says, Get Him Drunk (Master
    Cleanse–Tini), 82–83
Scents. *See* Perfumes
Scientific Certification Systems
    Greenhouse Gas Verification
    Program, 22–23
Scott, Laura, 199, 201–2
Scrubs, 36–37
Seafood/fish, 75, 190
Self-esteem, 28–29
Sex toys, 2, 160–68
Sexual health
    about, 108–9, 118–19
    Carnal Cleanse, 124–25
    exercise and, 112–17, 122
    men's imbalances, 122–27
    music and, 110
    nutritional issues, 111–12
    pharmaceuticals and, 109–10,
        117–18

Sexual health (*continued*)
  sexually transmitted diseases (STDs),
    129, 134, 137, 141–45
  women's imbalances, 119–22
Shoes, 62–63
Showers, 181–86
Simple Yellow Rice, 88
SIN (Substitute It Now!) list, 18–21
Skin Deep Web site, 13, 16, 18
*Skinny Bitch*, 74
Slow food approach, 68–69
Soap, 182–83
Soil Association, 24
Soy and soy silk fabric, 58
Spermicides, 131, 134
Sponge, the, 134
STDs (sexually transmitted diseases),
    129, 134, 137, 141–45
Sterilization, 134–35
Sulfates, 19
Sunscreen, chemical, 19
Sustainability, 4–5, 8–9
Swift, Rose-Marie, 42–43
Synthetic fibers, 59

T

Talc, 20
Tampons, 140–41
Tantric sex, 4, 157–59
Tencel fabric, 59
TerraChoice Environmental
    Marketing, 17–18
Terry, Bryant, 84
Toilet tissue, 17
Toluene, 20
Toners, 39
Tooth care, 40–41
Towels, 184–85

Toxic ingredients, 18–21, 27
Transparency, 13, 25–26, 29, 30
Transportation, 154
Tubes, tying, 134–35
*Two is Enough*, 199

U

*Urban Tantra*, 157
Ureas, 19
Urinary tract infections, 120–21,
    131, 142
USDA National Organic Program, 21

V

Vanilla Salad Starter, 77–78
Vasectomy, 135
Veganism, 73–74
*Vegan Soul Kitchen*, 84
Vegetarianism, 72–74
Viagra, 109, 117, 126
Vibrators, 160–61, 166
Vintage clothing, 55–56

W

Water, 181–82
Weddings, green, 196
*Well-Preserved*, 70
Wild carrot, 138–39
Wine, eco-friendly, 94–95
Wool, 57, 173, 177

Y

Yeast infections, 120–21, 143, 144, 145
Yellow Squash "Fettuccine" with Creamy
    Pine Nut Alfredo, 81–82
Yoga, 112–14
Young, Amanda, 155–56